Quill Pens and Petticoats

By the same author

Reading Shakespeare's Plays
An Introduction to English Literature

Quill Pens
and
Petticoats

A PORTRAIT OF WOMEN OF LETTERS

H. E. Stowell

WAYLAND PUBLISHERS LONDON

Copyright © 1970 by Wayland (Publishers) Ltd
Wayland (Publishers) Ltd
101 Grays Inn Road London WC1
SBN 85340 005 9

MADE AND PRINTED IN GREAT BRITAIN BY
THE GARDEN CITY PRESS LIMITED
LETCHWORTH, HERTFORDSHIRE

Contents

Introduction

In this small assembly are gathered together women of many different types and several centuries. The reader is invited to meet them as they can be seen in their own writings and in the opinion of those who knew them in their own time.

These are all remarkable women, for one must remember that until the nineteenth century most Englishwomen had little education, unless they were of the privileged classes who might be privately tutored or brought up in a convent. The usual role for a woman was that of wife and mother; nothing further was expected of her, whatever her own feelings may have been. But among the earlier writers were those like Margaret Paston, who found it necessary to keep in touch with her husband, whose business took him away from home in dangerous times. Naturally, letters, usually intended for one reader only, are the earliest and simplest forms of literary expression. They are powerful, direct and authentic.

Most of the women in this book, however, meant their work to reach the general public. The fact that they were women was an undoubted handicap. Several of them knew only too well that acceptance by publishers and public alike was much easier for a man than a woman. Some wrote under a man's name and later allowed their own identity to be revealed, as did Charlotte Brontë and Mrs Gaskell, but George Eliot, although her identity became known, continued to use her adopted name.

These word-portraits reveal something of the interesting human beings who lived and wrote, some in happiness and some in difficult circumstances, in the days before women had met men on equal terms in literature and art.

7

ONE

Julian of Norwich

ONE OF THE GREAT contrasts between medieval times and our modern twentieth-century world is the different attitudes towards 'signs and wonders', or 'visions and portents' as they were called. Today, with our knowledge of science and the physical world, we do at least look for the reasons for strange phenomena, even if we do not always understand them.

But in medieval days—Dame Julian's day—when the only educated people were in the monasteries or the few universities, most people felt any occurrence out of the ordinary was somehow significant. 'Signs from heaven' were warnings, taken as omens of some future event, even if, like the humble rainbow, they only meant that better weather was soon to come.

Many of the beliefs about the 'omens' in Dame Julian's day (1342-1443) were just plain superstition. Others, however, like rainbows or shooting stars, that had a basis in the Bible or Church teachings, were taken very seriously indeed. Whenever visions of angels or miracles appeared to good, even saintly people, the importance and influence that they had often reached far and wide through the land. In the space age of today it is hard to imagine the impact that such visions had. Pious men and women undertook long and difficult pilgrimages through the open countryside to meet those who had seen such wonderful things.

Dame Julian's was a lawless age, and the lawlessness of the country was reflected in a decline of standards in the Church. Bishops complained that even in some of the nunneries there were many nuns who had not learned how to read the services. Against

9

a dark background of poverty, plague, crime and illiteracy, Julian of Norwich spent a lifetime devoted to prayer and contemplation.

Yet her influence was enormous. Even today, though the Church is no longer united, learned people still think of her as a great English mystic and the author of one of the most beautiful works in Middle English.

She had just one outstanding spiritual experience and she wrote just one book, *The Revelations of Divine Love*. It gave a clear, direct acocunt of her Revelations themselves and of her understanding of them in the light of further meditation.

Little is known about her early life, however, except that she never set foot outside Norwich. Even her real name is a mystery, because when she decided to live an 'enclosed' life as an anchoress, or recluse, it was to the Church of St Julian that she went and it was from this that she took her religious name. She was certainly of good, probably noble family, and it is likely that she spent some years at the Convent of Carrow Abbey at Conisford, Norwich. It is not even known where the Revelations came to her; it could have been while she was at the Abbey, or while she was still living at home.

Julian tells in her book that she had always hoped and prayed for a vivid experience of the sufferings of Christ. Especially she hoped to be afflicted with three 'wounds'—contrition, compassion and a longing for God. This prayer was answered in the Revelations, or 'shewings', which came to her in strange circumstances on two successive nights when she was thirty years old.

As a result, she vowed to become an anchoress, and live for the rest of her life in her anchorhold in the Church of St Julian. This she did. Her 'hold' was a cell or small room at one side of the church, with another small room adjoining for her maid or helper. On one side a 'squint' window faced into the church and through this she could watch the services and receive the Sacrament. Another window faced outwards to the surrounding churchyard and through this Dame Julian spoke with the pilgrims who came day by day to tell her their many troubles and receive her advice.

Apart from her private prayer and meditation, this was her lifework, together with the writing of her book. When she was free to speak to her visitors she drew aside the black curtain with its white cross which covered the latticed window and was ready to help her 'even-Christians' (fellow-Christians). They came with both personal and general anxieties, for life was hard, taxes were high, poverty and crime rife and rebellions against tyrannical lords always on the point of breaking out. To all who came Mother Julian gave comfort to their souls, and, in her straightforward way, many practical suggestions.

One visitor who came in the early years of the fifteenth century was another famous mystic, Margery Kemp, who came from Lynn. She was not an anchoress herself but more of a traveller and teacher. She, too, had had some powerful visions and wanted to ask Julian whether they really came from God. Julian assured her visitor that the visions could be trusted so long as they did not suggest anything against the worship of God or the good of her fellow-Christians : 'God and the devil be evermore contrarious, and they shall never dwell together in one place; and the devil hath no power in man's soul. Holy Writ saith that the soul of a righteous man is the seat of God; and so, I trust, sister, that ye be. I pray God grant you perseverance.' So Margery went home to Lynn, reassured.

These words, written down at the time by Margery Kemp and quoted in her autobiography, illustrate the forthright language Dame Julian used to express her beliefs and give advice. The same simple and homely, almost brisk style, characterises her book, which is written in the current East Anglian dialect.

Two manuscripts lie today in the British Museum and in Paris, and were probably copied out by hand soon after Julian had written the originals. The first printed edition however, did not appear until the late seventeenth century. There are two versions of the book, one longer than the other, but both were probably written when Julian had spent nearly twenty years of her life wondering and praying about her original experience and finding fuller meaning in it as her devotion increased.

As she said, 'I had teaching inwardly, as I shall say.' She explained, 'When the shewing [revelation] which is given for a time, is passed and hid, then faith keepeth it by grace of the Holy Ghost unto our life's end.' She thought of her life as a spiritual journey, and wrote : 'I saw Him and I sought Him; I had Him and I wanted Him.' And after this I saw God in a Point, that is to say, in mine understanding—by which sight I saw that He is in all things.'

The simple, direct style in which the Revelations are written, reflect an orderly and logical mind. Julian was in the habit of putting her statements into three parts. The number three had great significance for her because the three-fold mystery of the Trinity—Father, Son and Holy Spirit—was at the centre of all her belief.

She was anxious to make it clear that there was nothing new in her Revelations, no new teaching but 'the common teaching of Holy Church, of which I was before enformed and grounded'. Nor did she ever claim any special virtue in herself because she had had Divine Revelations.

In one place she wrote : 'But God forbid that ye should say, or take it thus, that I am a teacher, for I do not mean that, nor meant I ever so. For I am a woman unlettered, feeble and frail. But I know well this that I say—I have it on the shewing of Him who is Sovereign Teacher—and truly, charity urgeth me to tell you of it ... *Because I am a woman should I believe that I ought not to tell you about the goodness of God, since I saw at that same time that it is His Will that it be known?'*

She begins the account of her sixteen 'shewings' by telling of her early prayer for three graces from God. The First Grace she wanted was 'To have mind of the Passion of Christ.' She longed to have been among those who had seen His suffering—'for I would have been one of them and suffered along with them'. To have a bodily sickness so severe that she could be emptied of all her own life and thus enter into Christ's suffering, was the Second Grace for which she prayed. And the Third Grace was 'to have God's gift of three wounds—Contrition, compassion and a wilful [conscious] longing for God.' Though the third prayer persisted the other two were forgotten until revived and answered by the Revelations in three ways : 'By bodily sight; by word formed in mine understanding; by ghostly [spiritual] sight.'

Before the 'shewings', however, came the preparation. 'In the year of our Lord 1373, the 8th day of May, when I was thirty years old and a half, God sent me a bodily sickness, in which I lay three days and three nights; and on the fourth night I took all my rites of Holy Church, and weened not to have lived till day. After this I langoured forth two days and two nights, and on the third night weened oftentimes to have passed; and so weened they that were with me.

'And being in youth as yet, I thought it great sorrow to die; but for nothing that was in earth that me liked to live for, nor for no pain that I had fear of, for I trusted in God of His mercy. But it was to have lived that I might have loved God better and longer time, that I might have the more knowing and loving of God in bliss of Heaven.'

She no longer felt pain. She now had an intensely clear sight and hearing of Christ's Passion. She described the bleeding Head and the scourged Body, the agony of the long drawn out suffering on the cross on a hill at Calvary, and then the sudden change in the Lord's appearance : 'And right in the same time that me thought, by the seeming, the life might no longer last . . . Suddenly He changed His blessed Countenance. The changing of His blessed Countenance changed mine, and I was as glad and merry as it was possible. Then brought our Lord merrily to my mind, "Where is now any point of thy pain or of thy grief?" and I was full merry.'

And later : 'Then said Jesus, our kind Lord : "It is a joy, a bliss, and endless liking that ever suffered I passion for thee; and if I might suffer more I would suffer more." '

Understanding the true meaning of His sacrifice, she says : 'A glad giver taketh but little heed of the thing that he giveth, but all his desire and his intent is to please him and solace him to whom he giveth it, and if the receiver take the gift highly and thankfully, then the courteous giver setteth at naught all his cost and all his travail, for joy and delight that he hath pleased and solaced him that he loveth. Plenteously and fully was this shewed.'

So she felt the humanity and the divinity of Christ revealed to her. It was followed, perhaps inevitably, by a dreadful vision of the devil : 'After this the Fiend came again with his heat and with his stench, and gave me much ado, the stench was so vile and so painful and also deadful and travailous. Also I heard a bodily jangling [loud talking] as if it had been of two persons, and both, to my thinking, jangled at one time, as if they had holden a parliament with a great busyness; and all was soft muttering, so that I understood naught that they said. And all this was to stir me to despair, as me thought.'

But '. . . All this sorrow that he [the Fiend] would make us to have, it shall turn to himself. And for this it was that our Lord scorned him, and this made me mightily to laugh. This, then, is the remedy, that we be aware of our wretchedness and flee to our Lord; for ever the more needy that we be, the more needful it is to come nigh to Him.'

But after the evil of this vision came the Consolation of Christ : 'It is sooth that sin is cause of all this pain; but all shall be well and all manner of things shall be well.' As if to emphasise this, it was repeated with an important addition : 'Thou shalt see thyself that all manner of things shall be well.'

Thus Julian came to believe that everything comes within the range of God's love, and the life of the soul, to her, meant a journey towards greater realisation of His presence : 'We are all in Him beclosed and He is beclosed in us. In nature we have our Being; in Mercy we have our increasing; in Grace we have our fulfilling.'

Julian rarely uses symbols, but when she does her pictures are very homely, she speaks of each soul as being like a child of whom Christ is the loving Mother, and writes of 'the homely loving of God'.

Another time she wrote : 'He shewed me a little thing, the quantity of a hazel-nut, in the palm of my hand, and it was as round as a ball. I looked upon it with an eye of my understanding, and thought, "What can this be?" And it was generally answered : "It is all that is made." I marvelled how it might last, for it seemed to me it might suddenly have fallen to naught, for littleness. And I was answered *in my understanding* : "It lasteth and ever shall [last] because God loves it." And so everything has its Being by the love of God.

'In this Little Thing I saw three properties : the first is that God made it; the second is that God loveth it; the third that God keepeth it.

'But what the Maker, the Keeper and the Lover are to me—I cannot tell; for till I am substantially oned [united] to Him, I may never have full rest nor very bliss; that is to say, till I be so fastened to Him that there is naught that is made betweixt my God and me.'

Although a very humble person, she was very sure how one should approach the Maker of the world. 'For our courteous Lord willeth that we should be as homely with Him as heart may think or soul may desire. But', she added, 'beware that we take not so recklessly this homeliness as to leave courtesy.' But 'prayer oneth the Soul to God', and 'In life is marvellous homeliness, and in love is gentle courtesy, and in light is endless Naturehood. These properties were in one Goodness; unto which Goodness my Reason would be oned and cleave to it with all its might.'

Although Julian was a mystic, she was still human enough to want to know the meaning of her visions; 'And from that time it was shewed I desired oftentimes to witten [know] what was our Lord's meaning. And fifteen years after and more, I was answered in ghostly [spiritual] understanding, saying thus :

' "Would'st thou witten thy Lord's meaning in this thing?"

' "Wit [understanding] it well."

' "Love was His meaning."

' "Who shewed it thee? Love."

' "What shewed He thee? Love."

' "Wherefore shewed it He? For Love." '

Ever humble, she felt sure she understood why the shewing had
been made to her : 'I am certain I saw it for the benefit of many
another, . . . I am certain there are full many who never had
shewing nor sight but of the common teaching of Holy Church,
and who love God better than I. For if I look at myself in particular I am nothing indeed.' She was to be a witness.

So this truly saintly woman, whose one desire was 'to love God
meekly, to dread Him reverently, to trust Him mightily', carefully
wrote down her message for succeeding generations. A message
best summed-up in her own words : 'It is God's will that we take
His behests and His comforts as largely and as mightily as we may
take them, and also He willeth that we take our abiding and our
troubles as lightly as we may take them, and set them at naught.
For the more lightly we take them, and the less price we set on
them, for love, the less pain we shall have in the feeling of them,
and the more thanks and need we shall have for them.

'He said not "Thou shalt not be tempested, thou shalt not be
travailed, thou shalt not be afflicted." But he said "Thou shalt not
be overcome." '

Her anchorhold was, with the rest of the ancient church of St
Julian, destroyed by a German bomb in the Second World War. In
the now rebuilt church a private chapel stands on the site of Dame
Julian's cell where two small portions of one of the stone walls
still stand in their original position.

Her medieval cell has gone; her book with its beauty and
sincerity remains.

TWO

Margaret Paston

IN THE MIDDLE YEARS of the fifteenth century, during the long, troubled days of the Wars of the Roses and for a time after they had ended in 1485, a regular correspondence was kept up by the members of a family of Norfolk landowners. This was the Paston family, who, so far from expecting their letters ever to be read by outsiders, often requested that the letter be burnt after it had been read. However, John Paston, after studying at Cambridge, became a lawyer, and in true legal fashion methodically filed away all letters for future reference. This practice was carried on by his sons until about 1509. The collection of letters was passed on down the family through the generations until, in 1729 the then head of the family, Sir William Paston, 2nd Earl of Yarmouth, needed some money and sold the letters to an antiquary. The letters changed hands several times and in 1787 their owner, William Fenn, published a selection of them, the first of many editions.

Their value as a record of the social and domestic history of the fifteenth century in immense. Completely spontaneous, they provide a valuable insight into the life of a prosperous, though not noble, land-owning family. Especially they are interesting in the way they show the impact of the civil war (Wars of the Roses) on such people. And though the majority of the letters are concerned with the family's business affairs yet requests for sugar, almonds or the money to buy some jewellery bring out the human, personal concerns of the writers, particularly the women.

The men of the family through their professional and business affairs, were often away from home, usually in London, for long periods at a time. Their wives were left in charge of their Norfolk houses and lands, and it is the wives who were the chief correspondents.

Agnes, wife of Sir William Paston, and her daughter-in-law Margaret, wife of John Paston, though entirely different in character were highly accomplished women. Both ran large households of indoor and outdoor servants and retainers, buying and selling the necessary land and farm stock. They also controlled the lives of their children, particularly their marriages, with zeal and affection and sometimes a severity that looks to us remarkably like cruelty. Both wrote regularly to their absent husbands, faithfully reporting all their doings and making anxious enquiries as to their husbands' welfare.

The letters begin about the year 1440 when Agnes Paston writes to her husband, Sir William, the head of the family, about Margaret Mauteby, with whose parents they have been negotiating the possibility of marriage to their son and heir, John Paston. The two young people have met for the first time and everything promises well:

'To my worshipful husband, William Paston, be this letter taken.

'Dear husband, I recommend me to you, etc. Blessed be God I send you good tidings of the coming and bringing home of the gentlewoman that ye weeten [know] of from Reedham this same night according to appointment that ye made there for yourself.

'And as for the first acquaintance between John Paston and the said gentlewoman, she made him gentle cheer in gentle wise and said he was verily your son; and so I hope there shall need no great treaty between them.

'The parson of Stockton told me that if ye would buy her a gown, her mother would give thereto a goodly fur; the gown needeth to be had; and of colour it would be a goodly blue or else a bright sanguine.

'I pray you to buy for me two pipes of gold [gold thread rolled on tubes or pipes]. Your stews [fish ponds] do well.

'Written at Paston in haste the Wednesday next after *Deusqui errantibus*, for default of a good secretary.

                          Yours, Agnes Paston.'
(Note : *Deusqui*, etc. are the first words of the Collect on the 3rd Sunday after Easter. Until the Reformation in the sixteenth century all prayers were in Latin).

So, with a new gown and a goodly fur, Margaret married John Paston and began a partnership which was a happy one. The business-like marriage arrangements were only characteristic of the time. As some later letters revealed, little or no account was taken of the feelings and wishes of the young people concerned.

It is clear from all Margaret's letters that she was prepared, as a wife, to devote herself entirely to the needs and interests of her husband and children and to regard her mother-in-law as her own mother. This, for her, was a labour of love. She never spared herself and was constantly and happily busy about family affairs which made increasing demands upon her as her children grew up. Her letters show her clear forthright mind, her practical common-sense, her determination and her versatility as well as affection.

In 1443, when her eldest son John was one year old: 'To my right worshipful husband, John Paston, dwelling in the Inner Temple in London, in haste.

'Right worshipful husband, I recommend me to you, desiring heartily to hear of your welfare, thanking God of your amending of the great disease that ye have had and I thank you for the letter that ye sent me, for, by my troth, my mother [her mother-in-law Agnes Paston] and I were naught in heart's ease from the time that we wist of your sickness till we wist verily of your amending.

'My mother behested [promised or vowed] another image of wax of the weight of you, to Our Lady of Walsingham and she sent four nobles [coins worth 6s 8d] to the four orders of friars at Norwich to pray for you; and I have behested to go on pilgrimage to Walsingham and in St Leonard's [at Norwich] for you; by my troth, I had never so heavy a season as I had from the time that I wist of your sickness till I wist of your amending and yet my heart is in no great ease, nor nought shall be till I weet that ye be very whole . . . I pray you heartily that you will vouchsafe to send me a letter as hastily as ye may, if writing be none disease [discomfort] to you, and that ye will vouchsafe to send me word how your sore do. If I might have my will, I should have seen you ere this time; I would ye were at home, if it were your ease, and your sore might be as well looked to here as it is there [where] ye be now, lever than a new gown if it were of scarlet.

'I pray you if your sore be whole, and so ye may endure to ride when my father [father-in-law] come to London, that ye will ask leave and come home, when the horse should be sent home again, for I hope ye shall be kept as tenderly here as ye be at London.

'I may none leisure have to do write half a quarter so much as should say to you if I might speak with you. I shall send you another letter as hastily as I may. I thank you that ye would vouchsafe to remember my girdle and that ye would write to me at the time, for I suppose that writing was none ease to you.

'Almightly God have you in His keeping and send you health.'

Adding a postscript :

'My mother greets you well and sendeth you God's blessing and hers, and she prayeth you, and I pray you also, that ye be well dieted of meat and drink, for that is the greatest help that ye may have now to your healthward. Your son [another John Paston, born 1442] fareth well, blessed be God.'

For some years Margaret and her mother-in-law lived in the same house and the two women seem to have had great respect and affection for each other. Various letters make it clear that Agnes, particularly after the death of her husband, Sir William, was a very dominating personality. A capable and vigorous person herself, she had small mercy on anyone who failed to live up to the high standards she set for them.

Margaret seems to have stood the test but Agnes's own daughter, Elizabeth, had to endure for many years her mother's anger and disappointment over the problems of her marriage.

When her son John, Margaret's husband, succeeded to the title and estates on the death of Sir William, the widowed Agnes wrote sending John his father's blessing and her own 'if that I find you kind and willing to the weal of your Father's soul and to the welfare of your brethren' [her other sons William, Clement and Walter].

Then followed good advice based on his father's precepts. He [John] should keep as far as possible out of the world of affairs : 'your father said "In little business lyeth much rest. The world is but a thoroughfare and full of woe, and when we depart there-from right naught bear with us but our good deeds and ill; and there knoweth no man how soon God will clepe [call] him; and therefore it is good for every creature to be ready." '

In 1448 a letter from Margaret to her husband John throws further light on both women. As do the majority of the letters it deals mainly with arguments with neighbouring landowners and threatened legal action about payments. Margaret had vainly tried to persuade a certain Lady Morley to wait for the settlement of some dues she claimed from John Paston until John himself returned home. Because of a difference of opinion about the rights of both sides Margaret wished to await John's arrival :

'I prayed her [Lady Morley] that she would vouchsafe not to labour against you in this matter till ye came home, and she said nay by her faith she would no more days give you therein; she said she had set you so many days to accord with her and ye had broken them, that she was right weary thereof; and she said she was but a woman, she must do by her counsel, as her counsel had advised so she said she will do . . . and I said I trusted verily that ye would do when ye came home as it longeth you to do, and if ye might have very knowledge that she ought of right to have it, I said I wist well that ye would pay it with right good will; and I told her that ye had searched to have found writing thereof, and ye could find none in none wise; and she said wist well there was writing thereof enough . . . and in no wise I could not get no grant of her to cease till ye came home.'

Notice the effect of the several negatives that denote the complete failure of Margaret's plea. However, next day, after hearing Margaret's story, her redoubtable mother-in-law Agnes went to Lady Morley, 'and she got a grant of my said lady that there should naught be done against you therein and ye would accord with her and do as ye ought to do, betwixt this time and Trinity Sunday'. After the serious business Margaret ends in a truly feminine manner, giving an account of a local wedding: 'The bride was to have much array of gowns, girdles and attires for her marriage to "the gallant with the great chain".' [This chain was probably a fashionable gold ornament].

The dispute with Lady Morley was only one of the many occasions on which we read of hard bargaining and skilful manoeuvring between property owners in days when, partly due to the changing fortunes of war, lands could change hands suddenly and often.

The letters trace in detail one dispute that affected the Pastons and a large number of other Norfolk landowners for many years. On the death of Sir John Fastolf of Caister Castle, John Paston, as one of his executors, inherited Caister but his ownership was often challenged, even though the family lived there for some time. Once, when the overlord of the district, the Duke of Norfolk himself, claimed the Castle it was actually besieged by troops. Margaret was living at Norwich then and John was in London trying to settle the lawsuits concerning all their properties.

At this time Margaret tells her husband that she recently learnt that his manor of Swainthorpe is directly held from the king, Henry VI, as part of a knight's fee [a holding in return for knightly service]. Therefore John must be ready at any time to send an armed man to Norwich Castle, at his own cost, for forty days and must also pay thirty shillings a year to the king.

In 1459 this was followed up by Margaret's news to John that he was one of several in Norwich to whom the king had sent a sealed letter requesting armed men for his cause to go to Leicester for two months. In John's absence his friends had advised her to allow her son, also John, to go instead. The young John had been very dutiful in oversight of the servants and in all other things 'the which I hope ye would have been pleased with and [if] ye had been at home; I hope he will be well demeaned to please you here-after . . . As for all other things at home, I hope that I and others shall do our part therein as well as we may; but as for money it cometh slowly and God have you in his keeping and send you good speed on all your matters.'

Henry VI, unhappy and ailing, was little more than a pawn in the struggle between the Lancastrian nobles of his party and the Yorkists headed by Edward Duke of York. Edward had become so powerful that in 1461 he had himself crowned as King Edward IV. Until then the Lancastrians had been constantly rallied by Henry's Queen, Margaret of Anjou, a brilliant and determined woman who, even after 1461, refused to accept defeat.

In 1452 she had visited Norwich, where Margaret Paston was living, to collect supporters. Margaret told her husband that she had been ashamed of her own jewellery when she met the Queen. She begged John to send her money before Whitsuntide 'that I may have something for my neck. When the Queen was here I borrowed my cousin Elizabeth Clere's device [ornament] for I durst not for shame go with my beads among so many fresh gentle-women as here were at that time.'

In an earlier letter she begs for 'a pot with treacle in haste, for I have been right evil at ease and your daughter both since that ye went hence [she and their daughter have both been ill] and one of the tallest young men of this parish lyeth sick . . . how he shall do, God knoweth'.

The same letter shows her constant concern for John's interests. She reports the death of a neighbouring knight, adding: 'If ye desire to buy any of his stuff, I pray you send me word thereof in haste and I shall speak to Robert Inglos and to Wichingham thereof; I suppose they be executors.' Yet despite her eager service Margaret was not always able to satisfy her absent husband in every particular. One letter humbly apologises for her 'simpleness'. 'By my troth, it is not my will neither to do nor say that should cause you for to be displeased and if I have done I am sorry thereof and will amend it. Wherefore I beseech you to forgive me and that ye bear no more heaviness in your heart against me, for your displeasure should be too heavy for me to endure with.'

After this plea the tone changes, she becomes brisk, and even a little short. John had evidently asked her to send him a number of things and to do some business on his behalf at home. She refers to 'the roll which was found in your trussing coffer [clothes chest]. As for herring, I have bought an horse-load for 4s 6d. I can get none eels yet . . . and as for all other errands that ye hast commanded for to be done, they shall be done as soon as they may be done.' With which promise she concludes.

However, John could relax occasionally in his letters and some time during the 1460s he wrote to Margaret in a gay mood calling her 'Mine own dear Sovereign Lady'. After asking her for material for making his winter garments and telling her what to do about items of property and deeds, he breaks into verse :

> Item, I shall tell you a tale,
> Pampyng and I have picked your male (opened your boxes)
> And taken out pieces five (money)
> For upon trust of Calle's promise we may soon unthrive,
> And if Calle bring us hither twenty pound,
> Ye shall have your pieces again, good and round.

> And look ye be merry and take no thought,
> For this rhyme is cunningly wrought.

> No more to you at this time,
> But God him save that made this rhyme.
> By your true and trusty husband.

Although the letters are mainly about personal and domestic matters there are many references to the uneasy and often dangerous situation in the country. In 1440 Margaret tells of foreign pirates coming into the bays of Yarmouth and Cromer : 'they have been so bold that they come up to the land, and play them on Caister sands and in other places, as homely [as much at home] as they were Englishmen; folk be right sore afraid that they will do much harm this summer but if [unless] there be made right great purveyance against them'.

Again in 1457 or 1458 in a letter to her son John, Agnes Paston tells of enemy raiders taking advantage of the civil war to harass the east coast. 'They took two pilgrims, a man and a woman, and they robbed the woman and let her go and led the man to the sea; and when they knew he was a pilgrim they gave him money and set him again on the land; and they have this week taken four vessels.'

The civil war brought dangers from their own countrymen and Margaret Paston asked John in London for weapons to defend their Norwich house against enemies. She wanted cross-bows, because long bows were useless to shoot out of the windows of such low houses, and poleaxes would also be welcome. How times have changed! Along with these formidable weapons there were some more homely requests: 'I pray you that ye will vouchsafe to do buy for me one lb of almonds and one lb of sugar and that ye will do buy some frieze [cloth] to make of your children's gowns. Ye shall have best cheap and best choice of Hay's wife, as is told me. And that ye will buy a yard of broadcloth of black for one hood for me, of 44d or four shillings a yard, for there is neither good cloth nor good frieze in this town. As for the children's gowns and [if] I have them I will do them maken.'

In the years 1459-61 there was much violence in the country. Margaret warned John to stay away from Norfolk as she had heard of a plot to kill him. She once told him that she was holding on his behalf twenty gold marks, the repayment of a debt, because she dared not send it to him as there were constant robberies on the roads between Norwich and London. (Not until Fanny Burney's time—the eighteenth century—did paper notes and bills really replace bullion.)

Even after the beginning of Edward IV's reign violence and lawlessness continued and Margaret was kept busy settling disputes among tenants, raising money and carrying on business under great difficulties.

In this she was not helped by her mother-in-law Agnes who, with advancing age, had grown even more masterful. She quarrelled with one local landowner after another with 'such great malice' that one confidential servant wrote to John, asking him to try to dissuade his mother from her violent attacks on her neighbours.

Although Agnes Paston was, in many ways, a difficult woman she seems to have been respected by her children whom she had to bring up alone after her husband's death in 1444. Margaret Paston was always anxious that her own children should show deference to their grandmother.

But Agnes's relations with her own daughter, Elizabeth, were not happy. Both hoped that a good marriage, from a business point of view, would resolve matters, but it was difficult to 'bring it to a good conclusion'. It was most important that the suitor should be one 'whose land standeth clear'. When such a man could not be found Agnes was so angry with her daughter that she refused to allow her to see any men, not even a servant, for many weeks. Worse than that, she had beaten her once or twice a week, sometimes twice a day, and had broken her head in two or three places. An elderly widower did propose marriage, but Agnes was not satisfied with his offers of money settlements and made difficulties.

Meantime, the kindly cousin, Elizabeth Clere, who had lent Margaret her neck ornament for the Queen's visit, wrote secretly to John urging him to bestir himself to find a suitable husband quickly for his sister for: 'sorrow oftentimes causeth women to beset them otherwise than they should do, and if she [Elizabeth] were in that case I wot well ye would be sorry; cousin, I pray you, burn this letter that your men nor none other men see it, for if my cousin, your mother, knew I had sent you this letter she should never love me.'

But Elizabeth did not marry for some time. She went as a paying guest to the household of Lady Poel, where she worried lest her mother should not pay promptly for her board. At last, however, she was betrothed to a man named Ponyngs and wrote to her mother Agnes about her 'best-beloved, as ye call him' whom she described as 'full kind to me, and is busy as he can to make me sure of my jointure, whereto he is bound in a bond of a thousand pounds to you, Mother, and to my brother John'. It is to be hoped that Agnes was at last satisfied.

Some time later when John and Margaret's daughter was growing up, Margaret told her husband that 'I was at Norwich this week and I was at my mother's and while I was there came in a kinsman of Elizabeth Clere's and he saw your daughter and praised her to my mother and said that she was a goodly young woman; and my mother prayed him for to get for her one good marriage if he knew any; and he said he knew one [who] should be of 300 marks [£200] by year . . . and he is of age of eighteen years old; if ye think it be for to be spoken of, my mother thinks that it should be got for less money now in this world [in the present state of affairs] than it should be hereafter, either that one or some other good marriage'.

Obviously the two women were eager to arrange a profitable

marriage for the girl while she was still quite young, although later events thwarted their plans.

This match-making has a strange link with modern times. In January, 1965 there was accidentally uncovered during excavations in London the coffin and skeleton of Anne Mowbray, daughter of the Duchess of Norfolk, known to the Pastons. In 1478 this child had, at the age of five, become the wife of Richard, second son of King Edward IV. Margaret Paston was interested in the way the widowed Duchess of Norfolk treated the king's proposal for his son. Anne would one day inherit great wealth and her mother spent a year holding out for concessions from the King. Finally he made the boy Richard Duke of York, and the Duchess of Norfolk then agreed to the marriage of the two children.

Margaret, like her mother-in-law and most women of those times in a similar position expected to have almost complete authority over her children as well as over her husband's home affairs. Time and again she reports in detail her transactions for him and their sons. Money became scarcer and her sons, the young Sir John [knighted in his father's lifetime] and the younger John must be found good positions in some nobleman's house and also make good marriages. Her husband must cultivate friends of the new king, Edward IV, who could use their influence on his behalf at court.

Her two sons both became members of the household of the Duke of Norfolk [of the Yorkist party] but when in 1470 Henry VI was restored for a short time to the throne they seem to have had no compunction about changing their allegiance.

An early letter from her son John begins : 'Most worshipful and my most special good mother, as humbly as I can recommend me unto you, beseeching you of your blessing.' This was his way of trying to get round her before saying what he really wanted, which was money and her supervision of his horse at home. How little has human nature changed!

On another occasion her letter reproves him firmly for not keeping his father and herself informed of his movements and for his spendthrift ways : 'It was told me ye sent your father a letter to London; what the intent thereof was I wot not but though he takes it but lightly I would that ye should not spare to write to him again as lowly as ye can, beseeching him to be your good father; and send him such tidings as be in the country there ye beeth, and that ye guard your expenses better than ye have been before this time ... I sent your gray horse to Ruston to the farriers and he saith he shall never be nought to ride, neither right good to plough nor to cart; he said he was splayed and his shoulder rent from the body. I wot not what to do with him. Your grandam [Agnes] would fain hear some tidings from you; it were well done that ye sent a letter to her how ye do as hastily as ye may and God have you in his keeping and make you a good man and give you grace to do well as I would ye should do.'

After the death of Sir John, her husband in 1466, Margaret was more anxious than ever about her family. She feared that John, the heir, would become involved as his father had been in the still unsettled will of Sir John Fastolf of Caister. She wrote: 'I advise you for to beware that ye keep wisely your writings that be of charge [legal documents] that it come not into their hands that may hurt you hereafter; your father, whom God assoil in his trouble's season, set more by his writings and evidence than he did by any of his moveable goods; remember that if they were had [taken] from you ye could never get no more such as they be for your part.'

She urges him to take the best possible advice about proving his father's will and to beware of several acquaintances who will try to claim certain properties from him.

A later letter of good advice about the estates ends in a way which gives us a glimpse of more homely matters: 'Also I send you by the bearer hereof closed in this letter five shillings of gold and pray you to buy me a sugar loaf and dates and almonds and send it me home; and if ye beware [spend] any more money, when ye come home I shall pay it you again . . . I pray you speak to Master Roger for my syrup; for I have never had more need thereof and send it me as hastily as ye can.'

A younger son John [not the heir but his younger brother] fought on the side of Henry VI at the battle of Barnet, and when he was wounded he wrote to Margaret: 'Now I have neither meat, drink, clothes, leechcraft [doctoring] nor money but upon borrowing and I have essayed my friends so far that they begin to fail now in my greatest need . . . Mother, I beseech you, and [if] ye may spare any money that ye will do your alms on me and send me some in a hasty wise as possible.'

This same John was very glad of his mother's good offices when he wanted to marry Margery Brews. The negotiations were left to Margaret and she and the bride's father had long arguments and discussions over land and money settlements. Finally both parties were satisfied and Margaret seems to have acquired a charming and affectionate daughter-in-law. Meantime, in a way that seems to us completely cold and calculating, she urged Sir John, as head of the family, to try to marry into the Woodville family, one of the relatives of Edward IV's Queen. In this way he might come to own more land and 'be set in rest'; 'at the reverence of God', she pleads, 'forsake it not if ye can find in your heart to love her'.

With this letter she sent some cloth of gold for John to sell in London to get money to pay for his father's tombstone, 'charging you that it be not sold to none other use than to performing of your father's tomb as ye send me word in writing; if ye sell it to any other use, by my troth, I shall never trust you while I live'.

A third son, Walter, was hoping to enter the Church and was sent to Oxford University with that in mind. Margaret wrote to a trusted steward : 'I pray you heartily . . . to bring Walter where he should be and to purvey for him that he may be set in good and sad [sober] rule, for I were loath to lose him, for I trust to have more joy of him than I have of them that be older . . . Write a letter in my name to Walter so that he do well, learn well and be of good rule and disposition, there shall nothing fail him that I may help with so that it be necessary to him; and bid him that he be not too hasty of taking [holy] orders that should bind him, till that he be twenty-four years of age or more, though he be coun- selled the contrary for often haste rueth. I will love him better to be a good secular man than a lewd [ignorant] priest.'

Walter did not become a priest. When he left Oxford he studied law and died before his mother at about the same time too (1479) as his grandmother, the redoubtable Agnes.

One member of Margaret's family received less patient treatment from her—Margery her daughter (not to be confused with her daughter-in-law, young John's wife, of the same name). This high- spirited girl actually dared to fall in love with a member of the Paston household, a retainer of some kind, named Richard Calle. The entire family disapproved of such a lowly suitor, but when Margaret accused Richard of deceit and trickery he retorted that he had shown his feelings openly. After that he and Margery married without anyone's consent and from their letters they seem to have been truly in love.

At once Margaret, backed up by her mother-in-law Agnes, tried to have the marriage contract annulled by the authorities. She wrote to her eldest son that she and her mother-in-law had been present when Margery was questioned by the Bishop of Norwich. Margery remained adamant and the bishop, not wishing to offend an influential family like the Pastons, delayed making up his mind.

Margaret was so angry that she ordered the servants not to let her daughter set foot in the house. So Margery went elsewhere and remained true to her love. Though this was a great grief to Margaret she was as determined as her daughter and steadily refused to see her.

There is no evidence in the letters that they were reconciled and Margaret did not live very long after this episode. It is quite possible that this zealous, over-burdened lady was more angry and unreasonable with her daughter than she would have been had she been younger and in better health. Indeed, Margaret's attitude to Margery in some ways echoes Agnes's treatment of her daughter, Elizabeth.

Margaret's letters reveal a very warm, human personality whose life was shadowed by the uncertainties and hazards of war and an unstable political situation in England. Like most women of her class and time her role was to devote herself entirely to her husband and family, who in this case seem to have taken more than they gave. But for someone who enjoyed organising, as Margaret obviously did, the influence such a woman had was quite considerable and certainly far more than that of women in Victorian days.

THREE
Dorothy Osborne

DOROTHY OSBORNE was the youngest member of the large family of Sir Peter Osborne of Chicksands Priory in Bedfordshire. She was born in 1627, in the reign of Charles I. Sir Peter was an ardent Royalist, one of the many who gave everything they had—and often their lives—to support Charles in his struggle against Parliament, both before and during the Civil War which broke out in 1642.

In that year Sir Peter, for twenty years Governor of the Island of Guernsey, was ordered by the Parliament Party to yield to them his stronghold there, Castle Cornet. He refused. He held out against a long siege and many offers of treaty until his health broke in 1646. Reluctantly, he wrote to Charles I asking to be relieved of his office so that he could retire with his wife and family to St Malo, there to try to recover his health, though not his fortune.

So it happened that Dorothy Osborne spent several years of her early life in France. Perhaps this fostered her love of French romances of which she became a great advocate in her letters. Thanks to the influence of some great friends, Sir Peter and his wife and family were able to return to Chicksands in 1649 but their means were limited and Sir Peter's health was ruined.

When Dorothy was twenty-one she and one of her brothers stayed at an inn somewhere in the Isle of Wight. Also staying there was young William Temple, son of Sir John Temple, a one-time supporter of the Parliamentarians. William, however, disliked the severity of the rising Cromwellian party, and was very pleased when young Osborne scratched a scathing comment on the Government on one of the inn windows. The three were promptly arrested but Dorothy, using the charm that later brought her many suitors, insisted that it was all her fault and, as she had hoped, they were soon released.

Thus began the love affair that was to be subjected to nearly seven years of trial and heart-ache, and end in a more than usually happy married life. William Temple and Dorothy Osborne soon had an understanding with each other but their respective fathers had definitely other ideas for them, and they knew that trouble would follow any suggestion of marriage. The entire Osborne family was fanatically Royalist and Dorothy, as the youngest daughter, was expected to marry some wealthy aristocrat. They considered Temple politically unsound and chiefly concerned with his own advancement. At the same time, Sir John Temple decided to send his son to spend some time becoming acquainted with life in various European countries. This travel, together with experience in London and in Ireland, where Sir John held office as Master of the Rolls, was an excellent way of acquiring that knowledge of men and affairs that made William Temple so useful in later life—in diplomatic missions abroad and in state affairs in England. He also studied widely and cultivated a pleasant style of writing, chiefly essays.

In 1652 William Temple returned to London from abroad and at once wrote to the girl at Chicksands; she in the meantime had resisted all other offers of marriage and had been, since their return from St Malo, devoting herself to her parents. Her mother died in 1652 and Sir Peter sank rapidly into feeble old age. The other usual member of their household was Henry Osborne who became more and more troublesome to his sister as by turns he cajoled and threatened her on the subject of her marriage to a suitable and wealthy husband.

But when she replied to Temple's first letter, Dorothy began a correspondence that lasted nearly four years. The lovers built up a written companionship that strengthened them both in their constancy. Only one of Temple's letters remains but Dorothy's, intended for his eye only, have given pleasure to countless readers since they were made available to the general public. The secret of their appeal lies largely in what she herself believed : 'all letters, methinks, should be free and easy as one's discourse; not studied as an oration, nor made up of hard words like a charm'. It is remarkable how little dated the letters seem; the writer's qualities as woman and writer shine out in all she says, and they are qualities that are never out of fashion.

As time passes and the letters are punctuated by rare meetings, it is easy to see how intimacy and understanding deepen. Before one brief meeting Dorothy wrote :

'But what an age 'tis since we first met and how great a change it has wrought in both of us . . . When we meet let us design one day to remember old stories in, to ask one another by what degrees our friendship grew to this height 'tis at.'

Her first letter, however, reveals much of her charm : 'And now, sir, let me tell you that I am extremely glad (whosoever gave you the occasion) to hear from you, since, without compliment, there are very few persons in the world I am more concerned in. To find that you have overcome your long journey, that you are well and in a place where it is possible for me to see you, is such a satisfaction as I, who have not been used to many, may be allowed to doubt of. Yet I will hope that my eyes do not deceive me, and that I have not forgot [how] to read; but if you please to confirm it to me by another, you know how to direct it, for I am where I was, still the same, and always,

Your humble Servant,
D. Osborne.

(The word 'servant' had two meanings in earlier English, the usual one, and a lover or suitor.)

On being reassured that Temple really was in London she writes : '. . . let me ask what you have done all this while you have been away, what you have met with in Holland that could keep you there so long; why you went no further; and why I was not to know you went so far? You may do well to satisfy me in all these. I shall so persecute you with questions else, when I see you, that you will be glad to go thither again to avoid me; though when that will be I cannot certainly say, for my father has so small a proportion of health left him since my mother's death that I am in continual fear for him, and dare not make use of the time he gives me to be from home lest he should at some time want such little services as I am able to render him. Yet I think to be in London in the next term, and am sure I shall desire it because you are there.'

This letter shows her affection, lively interest, and loving concern for her father.

Having told Dorothy all about his adventures, Temple had complained that she had told him nothing of her own life while he was away. She regaled him with an account of her various unwelcome suitors!

Of one she wrote: 'I had no quarrel to his person or his fortune, but was in love with neither and much out of love with a thing called marriage; and have since thanked God I was so, for 'tis not long since one of my brothers writ me word of him that he was killed in a duel, though since I hear that 'twas the other that was killed, and he is fled upon't, which does not mend the matter much! Both made me glad I had 'scaped him and sorry for his misfortune, which, in earnest, was the least return his many civilities to me could deserve.'

One of her most persistent suitors was an elderly widower with four daughters, all old enough to be her sisters. She was told by her friends that this Sir Justinian Isham was a man of great estates, of good breeding and famous for his wisdom. But Dorothy did not think much of him. She wrote, ' 'twas the vainest, impertinent, self-conceited, learned coxcomb that ever yet I saw . . . for his sake I shall take heed of fine gentleman as long as I live.'

But she could not resist the fun of imagining what it would be like married to 'Sir Solomon', as she called him. She suggested that if Temple was interested she would arrange for him to marry any one of her four step-daughters, and she herself would make him an excellent mother-in-law! Later she reported that Justinian, having tried several other suitable ladies, still preferred herself.

'Would you think it', she asks, 'that I have an ambassador from the Emperor Justinian that comes to renew the treaty? In earnest, 'tis true, and I want your counsel extremely what to do in it. You told me once that of all my servants you like him the best. If I could do so too, there were no dispute in't. Well, I'll think on't and if it succeed I will be as good as my word. You shall take your choice of my four daughters.'

Temple evidently laughed at this, but Dorothy soon tired of it and explained 'I find I want courage to marry where I do not like . . . I am clearly of opinion (and shall die in't) that, as the more one sees and knows a person that one likes, one has still the more kindness for them, so, on the other side, one is but the more weary of and the more averse to, an unpleasant humour for having it per-petually by one. And though I easily believe that to marry one for whom we have already some affection will infinitely increase that kindness, yet I shall never be persuaded that marriage has a charm to raise love out of nothing, much less out of dislike.'

Dorothy shows much common sense and determination. Other

suitors come and go, including a neighbour, 'a modest, melancholy, reserved man, whose head is so taken up with little philosophical studies that I admire how I found a room there, 'twas sure by chance; and unless he is pleased with that part of my humour which other people think worst 'tis very possible the next new experiment may crowd me out again'.

One of the least expected of her 'servants' was Henry Cromwell, second son of the Lord Protector of England, no less. He sent specially to Ireland for two large greyhounds for her, as she loved large dogs. There, however, it ended, though Dorothy assured Temple that she could have risen to greatness had she accepted the Protector's son.

She was always amused that sooner or later her rejected suitors found someone else to marry while she was left to 'wear the willow'.

'What a multitude of willow garlands shall I wear before I die; I think I had best make them into faggots this cold weather; the flame they would make in a chimney would be of more use to me than that which was in the hearts of all those that gave them me, and would last as long !'

Having watched many suitors over the years, she set out what she wanted in a husband for herself. Actually it was mainly a list of what she did *not* want :

'Our humours must agree; and to do that he would have the kind of breeding that I have had, and used that kind of company. That is he must not be so much a country gentleman as to understand nothing but hawks and dogs and be fonder of either than his wife; nor of the next sort of them whose aim reaches no further than to be Justice of Peace, and once in his life High Sherriff, who reads no books but Statutes and studies nothing but how to make a speech interlarded with Latin that may amaze his disagreeing poor neighbours and fight them rather than persuade them into quietness. He must not be a town gallant neither, that lives in a tavern and an ordinary, that cannot imagine how an hour should be spent without company, unless it be in sleeping, that makes court to all the women he sees, thinks they believe him and laughs and is laughed at equally. Nor a travelled Monsieur whose head is all feather inside and outside, that can talk of nothing but dances and duels, and has courage enough to wear slashes when everybody else dies with cold to see him.

'He must not be a fool of no sort, nor peevish, nor ill-natured, nor proud, nor covetous, and to all this must be added that he must love me and I him as much as we are capable of loving.

Without all this, his fortune, though never so great, would not satisfy me, and with it, a very moderate one would keep me from ever repenting my disposal.'

She must have watched and listened to many men she disliked. When Temple replied that she had merely written what she did *not* want, she answered that he already knew the kind of man she wanted to marry. She saw no reason to send him a list of his own virtues !

These comments on marriage, while they reveal her determination, her affection and her gay good humour, do not touch on the darker side of the picture. Medicine in the seventeenth century was very primitive. Dorothy was often ill and low-spirited. Like her father she suffered from 'fits' of ague. Shivering fevers, and the common cold seems to have plagued both her and Temple as often as it does today. She scolds Temple for being careless, sweating at tennis and then catching cold.

'Would anyone in the world but you make such haste for a new cold before the old had left him? In a year, too, when mere colds kill as many as a plague used to do? Well, seriously, either resolve to have more care of yourself or I renounce my friendship.'

Yet she has to confess to her own frequent colds, as here, 'I am so perfectly dosed with my cold and my journey together that all I can say is that I am here and that I have only so much sense left as to wish you were so, too. When that leaves me you may conclude me past all.'

She once sent him some of her cold medicine with the comment, ' 'Tis like the rest of my medicines; if it do no good 'twill be sure to do no harm and 'twill be no great trouble to you to eat a little ont' now and then.' She also refers to 'the spleen,' a nervous complaint for which she had to drink 'steel' water when she could not visit Epsom or Barnet mineral springs. She told Temple how she managed to drink the 'abominable' steel. He had asked her to think of him at a certain hour every day; she explained, 'I drink your health every morning in a drench that would poison a horse, I believe, and 'tis the only way I have to persuade myself to take it. 'Tis the infusion of steel, and makes me feel so horribly sick that every day at ten o'clock I am making my will and taking leave of all my friends. You will believe that you are not forgot then. They tell me I must take this ugly drink a fortnight and then begin another as bad; but unless you say so too, I do not think I shall. 'Tis worse than dying by the half.'

She usually tries to make light of her illness in her letters but once at least, her friend Jane had written to Temple saying how depressed and ill she had been. To his anxious inquiries she replied, 'Jane thinks nobody in good humour unless they laugh perpetually . . . which I was never given to much, and now I have been so long accustomed to my own natural dull humour nothing can alter it. 'Tis not that I am sad (for as long as you and the rest of my friends are well I thank God I have no occasion to be so), but I never appear to be very merry and if I had all that I could wish for in the world I do not think it would make any visible change in my humour.'

Her grief when one of her brothers died was great, but her feelings were further depressed by the heavy mourning clothes she had to wear. 'You never saw me in mourning yet; nobody that has will e'er desire to do it again, for their own sakes as well as mine. Oh, 'tis a most dismal dress—I have not dared to look in the glass since I wore it; and certainly if it did so ill with other people as it does with me, it would never be worn.'

During her father's last months of life she wrote, 'My father is now so continually ill that I have hardly time for anything. 'Tis but an ague that he has, but yet I am much afraid that it is more than his age and weakness will be able to bear; he keeps his bed and never rises but to have it made and most times faints with that.' She was so constantly in attendance that, 'I have had so little sleep since my father was sick that I am never thoroughly awake. Lord! how I have wished for you. Here do I sit all night by a poor moped fellow that serves my father and have much ado to keep him awake and myself too.'

Before those last sad days, she had had a more varied life. 'You ask me how I pass my time here. I can give you a perfect account not only of what I do for the present but of what I am likely to do this seven years if I stay here so long. I rise in the morning reasonably early and before I am ready I go round the house till I am weary of that, and then the garden till it grows too hot for me. About ten o'clock I think of making me ready, and when that's done I go to my father's chamber, from thence to dinner, where my cousin Molle and I sit in great state in a room and at a table that would hold a great many more. After dinner we sit and talk till Mr B. comes in question and then I am gone.

'The heat of the day is spent in reading or working and about six or seven o'clock I walk out into a common that lies hard by the house, where a great many young wenches keep sheep and cows, and sit in the shade, singing of ballads. I go to them and compare their voices and beauties to some ancient shepherdesses I have read of and find a vast difference there; but, trust me, I think these are as innocent as those could be. I talk to them and find they want nothing to make them the happiest people in the world but the knowledge that they are so. Most commonly, when we are in the midst of our discourse, one looks about her, and spies her cows going into the corn, and then away they all run as if they had wings at their heels. I, that am not so nimble, stay behind; and when I see them driving home their cattle, I think 'tis time for me to retire too.

'When I have supped, I go into the garden and so to the side of a small river that runs by it, where I sit down and wish you were with me. In earnest 'tis a pleasant place, and would be more so to me if I had your company. I sit there sometimes till I am lost with thinking, and were it not for some cruel thoughts of the crossness of our fortunes that will not let me sleep there, I should forget that there were such a thing to be done as going to bed.'

She constantly refers to their bad luck : 'I do not know that ever I desired anything earnestly in my life but 'twas denied me, and I am many times afraid to wish a thing merely lest my Fortune should take that occasion to use me ill. She cannot see, and therefore I may venture to write that I intend to be at London if it be possible on Friday or Saturday come sennight. Be sure you do not read it aloud lest she hear it and prevent me, or drive you away before I come.'

When her relatives, in mistaken kindness, warn her that she is growing old and it is her duty to the family to marry well, she writes, 'If you were but with me I could make sport of all this but "patience is my penance" is somebody's motto, and I think it must be mine.'

Other letters show this same patience : 'I agree with you, too, that I do not see any great likelihood of the change of our fortunes, and that we have much more to wish than to hope for; but 'tis so common a calamity that I dare not murmur at it; better people have endured it.'

But it was a different matter when her brother Henry made yet another attack on her defences. 'Next week my persecution begins again; he comes down and my cousin Molle is already cured of his imaginary dropsy and means to meet here. I shall be baited most sweetly, but sure they will not easily make me consent to make my life unhappy to satisfy their importunity. I was born to be very happy or very miserable, I know not which, but I am certain that as long as I am anything I shall be your most faithful servant.'

It was unfortunate for Dorothy that her brother Henry was so often at Chicksands; he even intercepted the carrier who brought Temple's letters at one time. Dorothy, however, arranged for them to be sent to the vicar of a nearby village and herself went to collect them. He, she reported on another occasion, was visiting Chicksands, talking to Henry about flying, 'and both agreed that it was very possible to find out a way that people might fly like birds and despatch their journeys so'.

Apart from her troublesome suitors and her over-zealous relatives, Dorothy had much to write about. She enjoyed, and knew that Temple would enjoy, gossip about various friends. A certain wealthy Mr Smith had broken off his engagement with one lady and been accepted by another. Dorothy comments, 'But à propos de Mons. Smith, what a 'scape he had made of my Lady Banbury; and who would ever have dreamt he should have had my Lady Sunderland, though he be a very fine gentleman and does more than deserve her. I think I shall never forgive her one thing she said of him which was that she married him out of pity; it was the pitifullest saying that ever I heard, and made him so contemptible that I should not have married him for that very reason.'

She was amazed at how many unhappy marriages she knew. 'What an age do we live in, where 'tis a miracle if in ten couples that are married, two of them live so as not to publish to the world that they cannot agree.' She believed that much friction could be avoided if wives were more patient and quiet, 'I have observed that generally in great families the men seldom disagree, but the women are always scolding.' She suggests that it would be a good idea if couples intending to marry were to live in the same house for some years of probation, 'and if in all that time, they never disagreed they should then be permitted to marry if they pleased, but how few would do it then!'

The letters do not often refer to the public events of the years in which they were written (1652-4); but when Cromwell suddenly overthrew the remnant of the Long Parliament by removing the Speaker from his Chair, and ordering the removal of the Mace, ('Take away those baubles!') Dorothy asks, 'But, bless me, what will become of us all now! Is not this a strange turn? ... Sure, this will at least defeat your journey. Tell me what I must think on't; whether it be better or worse, or whether you are at all concerned

37

in't? For if you are not I am not, only if I had been so wise as to have taken hold of the offer was made me by Henry Cromwell, I might have been in a fair way of preferment, for sure, they will be greater now than ever . . . If Mr Pim were alive again, I wonder what he would think of the proceedings, and whether this would appear as great a breach of the Privilege of Parliament as the demanding of the five members. But I shall talk treason by and by, if I do not look to myself.'

Dorothy, as a good Royalist, is comparing Cromwell's unconstitutional action with that of Charles I when he had entered an earlier session of the same Parliament (a thing no monarch can constitutionally do) to arrest five members whom he had accused of treason.

Dorothy was a devout Christian and her common sense and humour were a part of that devotion. She was quick to laugh at humbug :

'God forgive me, I was near laughing yesterday where I should not. Would you believe that I had the grace to go hear a sermon upon a weekday? In earnest, 'tis true; and Mr Marshall was the man that preached, but never anybody was so defeated. He is so famed that I expected rare things of him, and, seriously, I listened to him at first with as much reverence and attention as if he had been St Paul; and what do you think he told us? Why, that if there were no kings, no queens, no lords, no ladies, nor gentlemen, nor gentlewomen in the world 'twould be no loss at all to God Almighty. This we had over some forty times, which made me remember it whether I would or not.

'The rest was much at this rate, interlarded with the prettiest odd phrases, that I had much ado to look soberly enough for the place I was in that ever I had in my life. He does not preach so always, sure? If he does, I cannot believe his sermons will do much towards the bringing anybody to heaven more than by exercising their patience.'

Dorothy often recommended the books she had been reading, and the two lovers exchanged opinions about the French romances and the poetry—English and French—that both enjoyed. She had more time for books than Temple, and once, having offered to send him *Cleopatre*, which she had enjoyed, she breaks in, 'But what an ass am I to think you can be idle enough at London to read romances! No, I'll keep them till you come hither and here they may be welcome to you for want of better company.' She said once when there seemed to be a glimmer of hope for their marriage,

38

'Can there be a more romance story than ours would make if the conclusion should prove happy?' But there was still long uncertainty before her when she wrote thus.

She sometimes asks him to do a little shopping for her in London —some special seals for her letters, especially if they are Italian ones, with old Roman heads; orange-flower water and, in the middle of a serious recital of her 'persecutions', 'Did you not say once you knew where good French tweezers were to be had? Pray send me a pair; they shall cut no love.'

As the months of her father's illness dragged on (1653-4) the family campaign to arrange Dorothy's marriage was stepped up. Henry said she deceived herself in thinking that Temple had any great passion for her and he was so afraid of gossip and tittle-tattle 'amongst neighbours that have nothing to do but to inquire who marries and who makes love' that he even tried to arrange her marriage with a suitor of his own choice by a kind of remote control.

Dorothy had ways of dealing with all this: 'You are spoken of with the reverence due to a person that I seem to like, and for as much as they do know of you, you do deserve a very good esteem; but your fortune and mine can never agree, and, in plain terms, we forfeit our discretions and run wilfully upon our own ruins if there be such a thought. To all this I make no reply, but that if they will needs have it that I am not without kindness for you, they must conclude withal that 'tis no part of my intention to ruin you, and so the conference breaks up for that time.'

At the same time Temple was urged by his father to make a suitable marriage, and Dorothy knew what both their fathers must be feeling. Yet she promises, 'If ever I am left free and you in the same condition, all the advantages of fortune or person imaginable met together in one man should not be preferred before you.'

In the wintry chill of 1653 Dorothy was in the lowest depths of depression. Some of their letters miscarried, Temple had heard some gossip about her possible marriage and had evidently written reproaching her. In her misery she reproached herself for allowing their friendship to develop into stronger feelings; it had led to nothing but trouble for them both. She gave up hope and wrote: 'All I can do is to arm myself with patience, to resist nothing that is laid upon me, nor struggle for what I have no hope to get.'

He urges her to see him, but her reply is, 'You may do so if you please, though I know not to what end. You deceive yourself if you think it would prevail upon me to alter my intentions; besides, I can make no contrivances; it must be here, and I must endure the noise it will make and undergo the censures of a people that choose ever to give the worst interpretation that anything will bear.'

She explains that if she does see him, it must be for the last time. Only the most unexpected turn of fortune could possibly bring hope. She begs him to be sensible and let time help them both to forget what once they had been to each other. 'Think on't, and attempt it at least; but do it sincerely and do not help your passion to master you. As you have ever loved me, do this.'

As might be expected, he refused, and she writes again, begging him not to make himself ill with his feelings. 'Vent it all upon me; call and think me what you please . . . nay, I deserve it all, for had you never seen me you had certainly been happy. 'Tis my misfortunes only that have that infectious quality as to strike at the same time me and all that's dear to me.'

He is evidently furious with himself for adding to her misery and her reply to one letter says, 'I tremble at the desperate things you say in your letters; for the love of God, consider seriously with yourself what can enter into comparison with the safety of your soul? Are a thousand women or ten thousand worlds worth it? . . . If God had seen it fit to have satisfied our desires we should have had them, and everything would not have conspired thus to cross them.'

But a later letter brings again a tiny ray of hope: 'if I could have persuaded you to have quitted a passion that injures you, I had done an act of real friendship, and you might have lived to thank me for it; but since it cannot be, I will attempt it no more. I have laid before you the inconveniences it brings along, how certain the trouble is and how uncertain the reward; how many accidents may hinder us from ever being happy and how few there are, and those so unlikely, to make up our desires. All this makes no impression on you; you are still resolved to follow your blind guide and I to pity where I cannot help . . . I'll study only to give you what ease I can, and leave the rest to better physicians—to time and fortune.

'Here then I declare that you have still the same power in my heart that I gave you at our last parting; that I will never marry any other; and that if ever our fortunes will allow us to marry, you shall dispose me as you please; but this, to deal freely with you, I do not hope for.

'No, 'tis too great happiness and I, that know myself best, must acknowledge that I deserve crosses and afflictions but can never merit such a blessing . . . but from this hour we'll live quietly, no more fears, no more jealousies.'

Dorothy promised that she would let Temple know as soon as he could visit her at Chicksands. Meantime he must find something to do during the coming summer. 'Who knows', she writes, 'what a year may produce?' It seems that Sir John Temple, about to return to Ireland as Master of the Rolls, was willing to use his influence to obtain a post in Ireland for William, where he might even consider marriage with Dorothy. Temple hastened to Chicksands with the joyful news and it was secretly planned between them that as soon as he had found work in Ireland they would be married at once.

Dorothy could hardly believe that his visit had happened. She wrote : 'Lord, there were a thousand things after you were gone that I should have said, and now I am to write not one of them will come into my head. Sure as I live, it is not settled yet ! Good God ! the fears and surprises, the crosses and disorders of that day; 'twas confused enough to be a dream, and I am apt to think sometimes it was no more. But no, I saw you; when I shall do it again God only knows.'

Temple seems to have won over his father at last to agreement, if not enthusiasm, for the marriage. He busies himself in London in preparation for crossing to Ireland. Dorothy asks for and receives a lock of his hair and is also given a plain gold ring. Of the hair she writes, 'I am combing and curling and kissing this lock all day and dreaming on't all night.' There is something endearing about her exaggeration.

Almost as soon as Temple had left for Ireland, Sir Peter Osborne died and Dorothy mourned the loss of 'the best father in the world'. Before long she left Chicksands and went to visit various relatives in London and in Kent. It was in that summer of 1654 that Temple must have written from Ireland the only letter of his to be preserved. He wrote, '. . . believe me, whatever you have brought me to, and how you have done it, I know not—but I was never intended for that fond thing which people term a lover . . . For God sake write constantly while I am here, or I am undone past all recovery. I have lived upon them [her letters] ever since I came, but had thrived much better had they been longer'.

He feels very tempted to return to England, to see Dorothy and tries to persuade her to agree. He ends : 'For God sake let me know of all your motions, when and where I may hope to see you. Let us but 'scape this cloud, this absence that has overcast all my contentments, and I am confident there's a clear sky attends us. My dearest dear, Adieu.'

Dorothy, however, visiting in London, thinks he would do better to wait until his father was ready to return. She considers that he has as much duty to his indulgent father as he has to her. She was enjoying her visit to London. She gave Temple all the latest gossip about their aristocratic friends—their gay doings and various marriage arrangements.

She had even been told by one gossip that everyone knew that she (Dorothy) was engaged to a young widower, Lord St John, whom she had never even spoken to. This had amused her but she admits that if ever she hears Temple's name mentioned she finds herself blushing, and 'a blush is the foolishest thing that can be and betrays one more than a red nose does a drunkard'.

She was taken to fashionable parties, to masked assemblies at Spring Gardens and found herself much admired. However, in spite of these 'dangerous courses' she assures Temple that she is unchanged in her love for him. He had asked for a miniature painting of herself and although her courage failed every time she looked at herself in the glass she at last commissioned the well-known artist Cooper to paint her portrait for £15.

When she went to stay at the home of her brother-in-law, Sir Thomas Peyton, in Kent, she found little time to write letters. She described Sir Thomas, who seems to have acted almost as her guardian since her father's death, as very reasonable and kind about the idea of her marriage, provided he was properly approached, 'but when he is roughly dealt with, he is like me, ten times the worse for't'.

Of her life in his household she reported, 'we go abroad all day and play all night, and say our prayers when we have time'. She contrasted the full noisy household with the calm of Ireland. 'You, that live in a desolated country where you might finish a romance of ten tomes before anybody interrupted you, and I, that live in a house the most filled of any since the Ark.'

She was persuaded into acting a small part in a play; she found many of the visitors unpleasant and often drunk and her brother-in-law, although imperious and fault-finding with his family, did nothing to check their riotous behaviour. Fortunately she found two congenial fellow-guests, her eldest niece and a quiet widower.

At last the time of separation and unhappiness was almost over. Sir John Temple and his son returned from Ireland and a 'treaty' or contract of marriage was made by Sir John Temple and Sir

Thomas Peyton. Dorothy wanted her brother Henry also to sign the treaty. As she said, he truly loved her and had not opposed the marriage any more than Sir John Temple. When the marriage was finally settled Dorothy went again to London where she wrote short, lively, teasing notes that showed her high spirits to her lover whom she frequently saw in London. One short extract is characteristic:

'Well, my master, remember last night you swaggered like a young lord. I'll make your stomach come down; rise quickly, you had better, and come hither that I may give you your lesson this morning before I go.'

The wedding preparations were all made, the day approached and another blow fell. Dorothy went down with smallpox. She recovered, but her looks were spoilt by the facial scars that would always remain. There was no vaccination in those days. William Temple, however, was no mere lover of her beauty; his feelings were unaltered and the marriage took place as soon as possible. They began married life in Ireland, where for five years they lived with Sir John. When they returned to England in 1663, William (now Sir William) went to Brussels as English representative and later to The Hague where he helped make the Triple Alliance. Whatever he did, his life was shared by Dorothy who took a full and lively interest in all his political and diplomatic moves. One of these was the arrangement of the marriage of William of Orange to Mary, the heiress to the throne of England, (if the claims of the young son of James II were set aside, as indeed they were).

When William and Mary became joint King and Queen by the will of most English people, Sir William and Lady Temple continued to be among their intimate friends. Many letters passed between the Queen and Dorothy Temple but the former burned all her private papers shortly before her death so that nothing remains.

Misfortune still haunted Dorothy's life. Of their seven children only two survived beyond infancy. Of these a little girl later died of smallpox and the son, John having been appointed Secretary of State for War under William III, drowned himself in the River Thames, leaving a note to say he could not do the work he had undertaken.

But Dorothy's quiet strength and endurance and her love for her husband carried her through forty years of a marriage that, despite misfortunes, was happy in the truest sense. She died in 1695, aged 66. She and her husband, who survived her until 1699, were buried, with their children, in Westminster Abbey.

FOUR
Celia Fiennes

THIS REMARKABLE WOMAN made her contribution to literary history by keeping a detailed journal of her journeys on horseback through the length and breadth of England in the last years of the seventeenth century.

Accompanied sometimes by a friend, and sometimes by one or more servants, she travelled, often in real personal discomfort and even danger, on narrow, ill-made roads, many quite impossible for coaches. Over water-logged marshland, up and down stony precipitous hills and sometimes in thick mud, in rain or shine, she jogged along, as proud to record her mileage as any modern motorist.

Her account of these exploits was intended to entertain her many relatives, but her 'Introduction to the Reader' suggests that perhaps she dreamed of a wider public.

Although she wrote her *Journeys* in the first years of the eighteenth century, it was not until 1812 that a part of her manuscripts fell into the hands of Robert Southey, the poet and essayist, who quoted from it in a miscellany of his own, referring to her not by name but as 'A Lady'. The fuller manuscript was obtained later by Lord Saye and Sele, a descendant of the same family (Fiennes) whose daughter, Mrs Emily Griffiths, edited and published it in 1888 under the title *Through England on a Side Saddle in the time of William and Mary*. This time Celia Fiennes' name appeared on the title page.

Luckily for modern readers, an authoritative edition with some much-needed punctuation, explanatory notes and a helpful intro-

duction, was published in 1947 by Christopher Morris. In this
edition it is easy to appreciate the lively descriptions of English
people, places and customs as seen through the eyes of this adventurous spinster, whose spelling was as eccentric and variable as her
mind was eager for information.

Celia Fiennes was born in 1662, two years after King Charles
II's Restoration. She was the daughter of Colonel Nathaniel
Fiennes, second son of Viscount Saye and Sele, and so by birth
an aristocrat. She was also, by the long tradition of her family, a
Nonconformist or Dissenter in religion and a Whig in politics. She
was delighted when William III and his wife Mary II came to the
English throne in 1689, because it brought toleration for the Dis-
senters and a long period of political power for the Whigs.

Her father died when she was a child of seven and for many
years Celia lived with her widowed mother in their old home at
Newton Toney near Salisbury. It was from there that she undertook her first journeys, mainly visits to relatives who lived in
country houses in different parts of the country. She enjoyed not
only the company of her relatives and friends but also their 'seats';
she had access to an astounding number of magnificent houses, in
the days when they were really lived in. These she described with a
wealth of detail—rooms, pictures, statuary, furniture and hangings,
such as today are publicly on view to thousands of sightseers.

After her mother's death in 1691, she made her home chiefly in
London so that she could keep in touch with her sister. Despite
her noble birth her sister had married a wealthy merchant and
Celia was evidently very devoted to them and their family. She
admired her brother-in-law's business success as she admired everything that gave evidence of the nation's prosperity. It is clear from
her own observations that she had the qualities of a good reporter
—an unquenchable thirst for information, a determination to see
things for herself, a quick eye and ear, a photographic memory and
a sense of proportion. She enjoyed all her adventures and retailed
them with such gusto that the reader soon finds her an entertaining
companion and an ideal guide to the England of her day—to a
country whose entire population of four million was less than half
that of present day London.

She had a direct simplicity and commonsense; she knew what
she wanted from life, and usually found it. Wherever she went in
her journeys she insisted on seeing everything. Every church or
castle tower was climbed and the prospect from the top described
and the various mansions and villages below identified. Every

45

cavern was explored and its special features described in detail. She was never able to go down a mine, but she watched all that happened at the surface, and asked the miners many intelligent questions.

As a young woman Celia was not strong. She suffered from some form of rheumatism, and needed 'variety and change of aire and exercise'. She wished to divert her mind with 'those informations of things as could be obtained from inns *en passant* or from some acquaintance, inhabitants of such places'. A passage from her address 'To the Reader' (written probably in 1702) is given here in order to show that what she did for herself she warmly recommended to others, firmly believing in the benefits they would derive :

'Now thus much without vanity may be asserted of the subject, that if all persons, both Ladies, much more Gentlemen, would spend some of their tyme in Journeys to visit their native Land, and be curious to inform themselves and make observations of the pleasant prospects, good buildings, different produces and manufactures of each place, with the variety of sports and recreations they are adapt to, would be a souveraign remedy to cure or preserve from these epidemick diseases of vapours, should I add Laziness?

'It would also form such an Idea of England, add much to its Glory and Esteem in our minds and cure the evil itch of overvalueing foreign parts; at least furnish them with an equivalent to entertain strangers when amongst us, or inform them when abroad of their native Country, which has been often a reproach to the English, ignorance and being strangers to themselves. Nay the Ladies might have matter not unworthy their observations, soe subject for conversation, within their own compass in each country to which they relate; and thence studdy how to be serviceable to their neighbours especially the poor among whome they dwell, which would spare them the uneasye thoughts how to pass away tedious dayes and tyme would not be a burthen when not at a card or dice table, and the fashions and manners of foreign parts less minded or desired.

'But much more requisite is it for Gentlemen in general service of their country at home or abroad, in town or country, especially those that serve in parliament, to know and inform themselves the nature of Land, the Genius of the Inhabitants, so as to promote and improve Manufacture and Trade suitable to each and encourage all projects tending thereto, putting in practice all Laws made for each particular good, maintaining their priviledges, procuring more as requisite; but to their shame it must be own'd many if not most are ignorant of anything but the name of the place for which they serve in parliament; how then can they speake for or promote their Good or redress their Grievances?'

Her 'great pains' of rheumatism led her to visit nearly all the mineral springs in the country. She would go miles out of her way if she heard of another 'spaw' (spa). She went several times to Bath, Epsom and Tunbridge Wells and was quick to notice any improvements as these places became more fashionable. A favourite of hers in the North was Knaresborough with its neighbour Harrogate, the latter largely undeveloped but full of 'quick springs' running off various minerals and later to become a leading health resort. Sometimes, as at Bath and Knaresborough, she bathed in the waters and found relief. She always tasted the springs on her tongue, but only enjoyed drinking those which bubbled up strongly into clean stone 'basons'. Anything sluggish or clouded she thought could not be beneficial.

Of the town of Bath she writes: 'The town lies low in a bottom and its steep ascents all ways out of the town; the houses are indifferent, the streets of a good size well pitched; there are several good houses built for Lodgings that are new and adorned and good furniture, the baths in my opinion makes the town unpleasant, the aire thicke and hot by their steem, and by its own situation so low encompassed with high hills and wood.'

She paints a picture of the various baths and the treatment available. We have room for only one extract here, but the whole account is instructive and entertaining:

'There are such a number of Guides to each bath, of women to waite on the ladyes and of men to waite on the gentlemen, and they keepe their due distance; there is a Serjeant belonging to the baths that all the bathing tyme walkes in galleryes and takes notice order is observed, and punishes the rude, and most people of fashion sends to him when they begin to bathe then he takes particular care of them and complements you every morning, which deserves its reward at the end of the Season.

'When you would walk about the bath I use to have a woman guide or two to lead me, for the water is so strong it will quickly tumble you down; and then you have 2 of the men guides goes at a distance about the bath to cleare the way; at the sides of the Arches are rings that you may hold by and so walke a little way, but the springs bubbles up so fast and so strong and are so hot up against the bottoms of one feete, especially in that they call the Kitching in the K[ings] bath, which is a great Cross with seates in the middle and many hot springs riseth there; the Kings bath is very large, as large as the rest put together, in it is the hot pumpe that persons are pumpt at for lameness or on their heads for palsyes; I saw one pumpt, they put on a broad brim'd hatt with the crown cut out, so as the brims cast off the water from the face; they are pumpt in the bath; one of the men Guides pumps, they have two pence I thinke for 100 pumps, the water is scallding hot out of the pump, the armes or legs are more easily pumped.

'The Ladyes goes into the bath with garments made of a fine yellow canvas, which is stiff and made with great sleeves like a parsons gown, the water fills it up so that its borne off that your shape is not seen, it does not cling close as other linning which lookes sadly in the poorer sort that go in their own linning.'

Knaresborough 'spaw'—a holy well—was a complete contrast to Bath. There she bathed in 'exceeding' cold water which helped to relieve ' a great paine I used to have in my head'. Like many other people, she was sure that the cold water prevented the catching of colds because it 'shuts up the pores of the body'.

Of Epsom she once reported : 'the well is timber-covered and is so darke you can scarce look down into it for which cause I do dislike it; its not a quick spring and very often it is dranke drye, and to make up the deficiency the people do often carry water from common wells to fill this in a morning (this they have been found out in) which makes the water weake and of little opperation unless you can have it first from the well before they can have put in any other'.

But fascinating as she found the 'spaws' they were not the chief objects of her travels. She had a lifelong interest in all the works of man, and a critical appreciation of his activities. Well-planned towns with broad streets and fine public buildings, filled with busy people producing goods of many kinds delighted her heart. These she found in many parts of the country—Bristol with its harbour full of ships and Exeter, as famous for its serges as Norwich was for calico and damask.

She found that the whole district for twenty miles around Exeter was employed in 'spinning, weaving, dressing, scouring, fulling and drying 'the serges', it turns the most money in a weeke of anything in England, one week with another there is 10,000 pound paid in ready money'. She admired everything in Exeter yet had to admit- that as she watched the serges being processed the smell of oil and grease was horrible. She praised Newcastle-on-Tyne as 'a noble town and most ressembles London of any place in England'.

She had, however, already paid a similar compliment to Liverpool where she found good streets and well-dressed people, 'London in miniature as much as ever I saw anything'. At Gloucester— 'a low, moist place by the Severn, where one must travel on causseys'—she admired the variety of knitted cotton goods that was made—'stockings, gloves, waistcoats and petticoats'. This she also found at Nottingham—one of her favourite towns—while Canterbury's flourishing trade in the weaving of flowered silks, 'very good ones', interested her as much as the beauties of the Cathedral. She describes again the whole process of hand weaving and also the paper-making from 'raggs' that she watched in a nearby watermill.

Another prosperous place she enjoyed was Leeds, 'esteemed the wealthiest town of its bigness in the country, its manufacture is the woollen cloths in which they are all employed and are esteemed very rich and very proud, they have provision so plentifull that they may live with very little expense and get much variety . . . there is still this custom on a market day at the bridge at the sign of the Bush just by the bridge anybody that will goe and call for one tanckard of ale and a pinte of wine and pay for these only, shall be set to a table to eate with 2 or 3 dishes of good meate and a dish of sweetmeates after'.

She comments, 'had I known this and the day which was their Market I would have come then but I happened to come a day after the Market, however, I did only pay for 3 tanckards of ale and what I eate and my servants was gratis'.

At Coventry she not only praised their 'thriving good trade' but the uses to which they put public money—'they have a great public stock belonging to the Corporation, above three thousand pounds a year for public schools, charity and the maintenance of their several public expenses'. Here, as in many other places, she found a story to enliven her account—here it was of Lady Godiva and Peeping Tom, 'the statue of a man looking out of a window with his eyes out'.

A staunch Dissenter, Celia was always happy in the various towns she visited to find popular 'meeting-houses' where she worshipped on Sundays. Yet she never failed to enjoy the great Cathedrals—she must have visited nearly all of them—and the ancient castles, not that she much cared for ruins. She disliked anything that was not 'neate'—a favourite word meaning soundly constructed, well shaped and good to look at. She described the house of one of her young newly-wed relatives as 'a little neate box'. Any town or building, whether castle or cottage, that was 'ruinated' she deplored. Dirt and neglect to her meant laziness.

On her great Northern Journey she crossed into Wales and Scotland. Both displeased her: 'at Holly Well [Holywell] they speake Welshe, the inhabitants go barefoote and bare-leg'd, a nasty sort of people'; and of Scotland : 'The Borderers seem to be very poor people which I imparte to their sloth.' She instanced '2 or 3 great wenches as tall and bigg as any women who sat hovering between their beds and the chimney-corner all idle doing nothing or at least was not settled to any work, tho' it was nine of the clock when I came thither, haveing gone 7 long miles that morning'.

She was disgusted by the small houses filled with smoke : there were no chimneys and the fumes had to escape through holes in the walls. She found this so nauseating that she went off to the stable to join her horse and smell the hay. She refused all food, but enjoyed instead some excellent claret straight from France and freshly tapped for her. She was a connoisseur of wine and ale and had a hearty appreciation of good food. In every town, she looked out for special local dishes—Cornish apple pie topped with a creamy custard, Colchester oysters (though far too dear) and York Cod and Salmon. She usually drank ale; the pale, clear ale at Nottingham was the finest she ever tasted, because it was stored in cellars carved out of the rocks on which the Castle stood. Characteristically she found her way down to the cellars to see and taste for herself.

She loved to see food displayed in the open markets held in many towns and often made her own purchases with a shrewd eye for a bargain. In Ripon market she saw 'a good quarter of lamb for 9 or 10 pence and two good shoulders of veal, one for 5 pence, the other 6 pence, and a quarter of Beef for 4 shillings and Crawfish 2 pence a dozen so we bought them; notwithstanding some of the Inns are very dear to Strangers they can impose on'. She much disliked such treatment for she was a shrewd and thrifty woman despite her easy circumstances.

She lost her temper at Carlisle, for 'there is a large Market place with a good Cross and Hall and is well supplied as I am informed with provisions at easye rates, but my Landlady, notwithstanding, ran me up the largest reckoning for almost nothing; it was the dearest lodging I met with and she pretended she could get me nothing else, so for 2 joynts of mutton and a pinte of wine and bread and beer I had a 12 shilling reckoning; but since, I find tho' I was in the biggest house in town I was in the worst accommodation and so found it, and a young giddy Landlady that could only dress fine and entertain the soldiers'. She could be severe when people or places were below her own standards.

Mansfield is quickly dismissed : 'there is nothing remarkable here but the dearness of the Inns, though in so plentiful a country', while Dover, apart from its Castle, which she greatly admired with its '120 steps to the Tower, whence you may discover Callice [Calais] in France; I saw the hills and clifts plain', was described thus : 'it looks like a place of no deffence, its a little place, the houses are little and look thrust together; there is no market house and town hall, its well enough for the accommodation of the seamen and to supply the ships with anything.'

The City of York, she complained, 'makes but a mean appearance; the steets are narrow and not any length save one which you enter from the bridge that is over the Ouse', but the 'noble minster' satisfied her completely; she examined it inside and out from the topmost tower with its wonderful 'prospect' for miles around to the Chapter house where there was a Mint at work, 'coining the old money and plate into new, milled money. I saw them at work and stamped one half-crown myself'. Even she was not, however, allowed to see the milling of the edges, 'which Art they are sworn to keep secret'.

As with York, so with Chester, our traveller was full of admiration for the Cathedral and enjoyed walking on the old City walls but objected to the famous Rows because 'these penthouses darken the streetes and hinder the light of the houses in many places to the streetward below'. Glastonbury Church tower revealed a prospect of the town 'which appeared very ragged and decayed' while St Albans Cathedral was 'so worn away that it mourns for some charitable person to repair it'.

Her severest censure was reserved for Ely where 'the Fens are full of water and muddy'. She had a good view of the Cathedral as she went across the dykes on a gravel 'causey' (sometimes she spells it 'caussey'), causeway or narrow track, and she had one of her several lucky escapes here. Owing to heavy rain the Causey was under water, 'and a remarkable deliverance I had, for my horse, earnest to drinke ran to get more depth of water than the Causey had, was on the brinke of one of these diks [dykes] but by a special providence which I desire never to forget and allwayes to be thank-full for, escaped'.

The greater part of Ely was 'the dirtyest place I ever saw . . . a perfect quagmire the whole Citty'. Her bedroom there 'was near 20 stepps up, I had froggs and slow-worms and snailes in my roome, but suppose it was brought up with the faggots, but it cannot but be infested with all such things being altogether moorish fenny ground which lyes low; its true were the least care taken to pitch their streets it would make it looke more properly an habitation for human beings and not a cage or nest of unclean creatures'.

She reproaches the Bishop who is Lord of the whole Island for spending so little time in the place and declares that the people themselves are lazy. She had ideas of her own as to how the fens could be properly drained instead of wasting at least £3,000 a year on draining and repairing the banks of the dykes. But she believed the people to be too lazy to accept any plan, however good.

It was not only in the Fens that the going was difficult in those days. In the Midlands she took nearly eleven hours to go twenty-five miles. 'A footman here could have gone much faster than I could ride, for it was all full of sloughs and wet clay.' In Lancaster her horse fell down on his nose because of the wet, slippery stones 'but did at length recover himself and so I was not thrown off or injured, which I desire to bless God for, as for the many preserva-tions I met with'. And yet again on her way from Newton Toney to Windsor she found the chalky, unmade roads slippery after rain. Her horse's feet failed and 'he could noe ways recover himself and so I was shot off his neck upon the bank, but noe harm I bless God, and as soon as he could role himself up stood stock still by me, which I looked on as a great mercy'.

On one southern journey after seeing all the beauties of Ply-mouth—the harbour and docks, the Citadel and the fine house at Mount Edgcumbe ('esteemed by me the finest seat I have seen, and might more rightly be named Mount Pleasant')—she went across by ferry boat into Cornwall. She described the crossing as very dangerous : 'I was at least an hour going over; it was about a mile, but indeed in some places notwithstanding there was 5 men rowed and I sett my own men to row alsoe, I do believe we made not a step of way for almost a quarter of an hour . . . but those ferry boats are soe wet and then the sea and wind is allways cold to be upon, that I never faile to catch cold in a ferry-boate as I did that day'.

She recorded an unpleasant experience with some rough men who rushed out from the nearby thickets upon her little party, jostled their horses and seemed about to attack them; but she took the rough with the smooth and the only emotion she expressed is gratitude for her safety in such lawless times. Only once did she call a halt to her adventurous spirit. At Land's End she was only two days' sail from France, 'but the peace being but newly entred into with the French, I was not willing to venture, at least by myself, into a Forreign Kingdom, and being then at the end of the land my horses leggs could not carry me through the deep and so returned again to Persands' [Penzance]. So with a small joke she turned her back on France.

Such were some of the experiences of an early woman traveller among the roads and cities of pre-Industrial England. She had a passionate interest in the mineral wealth of the country; she marvelled at the rich supplies of marble 'both black and white, rance and curiously veined and polished' which had gone to make the floors and chimney-pieces of Chatsworth Hall.

The store of copper, tin and lead intermixed with silver redeemed the bleak, steep hills of Derbyshire in her eyes, 'for though the surface of the earth looks broken, yet these hills are impregnated with rich marbles, stones, metals, iron and copper and coal mines in their bowels, from whence we may see the wisdom and benignity of our great Creator to make up the deficiency of a place by an equivalent as also the diversity of the Creation which increaseth its beauty'.

The salt mines of Cheshire and the salterns of Lymington, where the salt was evaporated from sea water, fascinated her too, and she made careful notes of the process. She knew a good deal about coal and visited local mines whenever she could. In Chesterfield she wrote, 'they make their mines at the Entrance like a well and so till they come to the coale, then they digg all the ground about where there is coale and set pillars to support it and so bring it to the well, where by a basket like a hand-barrow by cords they pull it up; so they let down and up the miners with a cord'.

She quickly learned about the different kinds of coal and the purposes for which they were suitable. The shining 'cannal coale' from Lancashire and Staffordshire splits easily and 'burns as light as a candle—set the coales together with some fire and it shall give a snap and burn up light'; the 'sea-coale' carried by sea from New-castle-on-Tyne was the kind that cakes and 'is common and familiar to every smith in all villages'.

53

When paying a visit to the caves at Buxton, she noted the strange shapes carved out by the constantly dropping water. She heard the famous 'ecchoe', and 'as I went I clambered over the top of all the stones and as I came back I pass'd under several of the arches like bridges'. The fluor-spar of Buxton seemed to her 'like crystal or white sugar candy, it's smooth like glass but it lookes all in cracks all over'. At Bristol she saw the 'Bristol diamonds' in the rocks of the Avon gorge. She brought back a souvenir, a piece 'just as it came out of the rock with the rock on the backside and it appeared to me as a cluster of diamonds polish'd and irregularly cut'.

Although her practical nature was always attracted by the resources of a place and the use made of them, she was not insensitive to the beauty of the countryside. In an age of bad roads, most people had little idea of conditions far from their own homes, and travel was a constant wonder.

After visiting Yorkshire where the steepness of the hills amazed her she crossed over the Pennines into Lancashire by Blackstone Edge and went down into the valley. It seemed to her like a miniature of the Alps of which her Father had told her stories as a child, 'soe though on the top it hold snow and haile falling on the passengers which at length, the lower they go, comes into raine and so into sunshine at the foote of those valleys fruitful the sunshine and singing of birds'.

But scenery attracted her less than well cultivated gardens. On visits to country houses, she always investigated the gardens and greenhouses. Her knowledge of plants was extensive and she writes of them with obvious pleasure. She marvelled at an Italian pomegranate tree: 'it was as tall as myself, the leafe is a long slender leafe of a yellowish greene edged with red and feeles pretty thick, the blossom is white and very double'; in the 'Physick Garden' at Oxford, 'the variety of flowers and plants would have entertained one a week'. Everything was in the Italian fashion. She breaks her account of the gardens at Woburn Abbey to confess 'I eate a great quantity of the Red Coraline Goosbery which is a large, thin-skin'd goosebery' (her spelling was inconsistent!).

Something must be said of her visits to Oxford and Cambridge. At Oxford particularly, she took pride in her ancestry. She could claim New College as 'ours' because it belonged, as did Winchester School, to her family who were Wykeham-Fiennes by descent from the sister of William of Wykeham, the founder of Winchester. Celia was therefore 'Founder's Kin' at both places. Several times

she made an extensive tour of the colleges, libraries and gardens—
indeed, Trinity College was completed between two of her visits.

The highlight of Cambridge for her, as for most other visitors,
was King's College Chapel. She has high praise for other Colleges
and their gardens, also 'the Library farre exceeds that of Oxford'.

One journey to London took her through Windsor where the
splendours of the Castle and St George's Chapel were a worthy
challenge to her descriptive powers. The twenty-six knights who,
today as then, hold the highest honour bestowed by the monarch
were called 'the honourable Order of the Blew Garter'. She
describes the banners and ensigns of 'the severall knights', their
special stalls in the Chapel of St George and their ceremonial
robes, familiar to many people today, but only for the very few
until modern inventions brought their pictures before the public.
She mentions the blue velvet capes and the 'blew Garter in which
hangs a George on horseback besett with jewels and a diamond
Garter put on their right leg'.

The view from the tower at Windsor Castle charmed her with
'the great prospect of the whole town and Winsor Forrest and the
country round to Kensington; I could see my Lord of Holland's
house and rowes of trees and to Harrow of the Hill, and to Shooters
Hill beyond London!' She also saw several noblemen's houses, the
Long Walk and 'the river Thames which twists and turns it self
round the meddowes and grounds'.

She had a flair for seeing small things as well as 'prospects':
'upon this tower which is most tymes moist, all in the walls grows
the best maiden haire, both white and black, which is an herb
much esteemed for coughs and to put into drinks for consump-
tions.' Such was eighteenth-century medicine!

Later, she went to Windsor Forest to watch a race between an
Englishman and a Scotsman on a round track of four miles; this
they had to cover to make up 22 miles—the distance from Charing
Cross to Windsor Cross. It took them two and half hours in all.
'The English [man] gained the second round the start and kept it
at the same distance the five rounds and then the Scotchman came
up to him and before him to the post; the English man fell down
within a few yards of the post; many hundred pounds were won
and lost about it, they ran both very neatly but my judgement gave
it to the Scotchman because he seemed to save himself to the last
push.'

Too old by now to journey far, she still always kept her eyes
open for anything of interest.

Celia Fiennes always made a note of her total mileage for the year, including the extra journeys on shorter visits. In 1697 when she had made her Northern Journey and a shorter one into Kent, she writes that her year's total 'besides the little ridings to take the aire at the parke' was about 1,045 miles 'of which I did not go above a hundred in the coach'.

But by 1702 her long journeys had come to an end. She settled in London and there, using the copious notes she must have made, she began to write her book. London, however, provided her with fresh material; here she was at the heart of England and she must needs write, expansively as ever, of the composition and government of the City of London, 'the Citty properly for trade' and of Westminster 'the Citty for the Court'. She describes the pageantry of the Lord Mayor's Show, the activities of the Companies or Trade Guilds; she describes the triumphal return of King William III after making peace in Europe, his reception by the Lord Mayor of London and all the dignitaries who rose out to greet him, 'all which paid their respective homage and duty to the King, who receiv'd it very kind and obligingly as he did the generall joy and acclamations which proceeded from thousands which were spectators; at Paul's Schoole the scholars made him a speech and thus he was conducted to his own pallace at Whitehall'. Whitehall, with the exception of the Banqueting Hall, was burnt down the following year (1698).

In the same year she reports that St Paul's Cathedral was almost rebuilt after its destruction by fire in 1666. The Dome was not yet in place and the great building was being paid for by a tax on coals in London.

She witnessed many great state occasions in Westminster Hall and Westminster Abbey. Mary II died in 1694 and her husband William III in 1702. Celia Fiennes was a 'mournful spectator or hearer of two of the most renowned funerals that ever was'. She reports that the Queen's remains 'lay in State in Whitehall in a bed of purple velvet all open', the cannopy the same with rich gold fring' and all the panoply of state is enumerated. The body was later shrouded in black and carried to the Abbey for the burial service.

She was delighted to attend the coronation of Queen Anne. Her mastery of the elaborate ritual and ceremony and her detailed description of colourful robes and jewels would have certainly made her an outstanding radio commentator today.

The Queen passed from Westminster Hall to the Abbey 'under a

56

large canopy carried by 16, and she because of lameness of the gout had an elbow chair of crimson velvet with a low back by which means her mantle and robe were cast over it and borne by the Lord Master of the Robes and the first Duchess and so on to the rest of her train and attendants'. She left the chair at the Abbey doors and walked in.

'Her head was well dress'd with diamonds mixed in the haire which at the least motion brill'd and flamed; she wore a crimson velvet cap with ermine under the circlet which was set with diamonds and on the middle a sprig of diamond drops transparent hung in form of a plume of feathers, for this cap is the Prince of Wales's cap which till after the Coronation that makes them legall king or queen they wear.'

At the banquet held afterwards in Westminster Hall our commentator reports that the Queen should have sat on the dais in lonely splendour at a table under her canopy. Instead, she invited her husband Prince George of Denmark to sit at table with her (though not under the canopy). This honour to a mere consort seems to have caused something of a sensation.

Westminster Hall was also the scene of the proceedings of the Courts of Justice and Celia gives an excellent account of the functions of the different courts and the distinction between Common and Civil Law. She denounces the courts of her time as corrupt and dilatory, scandalised by greedy lawyers and ruined plaintiffs and defendants. Yet she writes quite calmly about the punishments of her time—the hanging of prisoners at Tyburn, 'drawn thither in a cart with their coffin tied to them and halters about their necks'. Those convicted of high treason had no coffins because they were hanged, drawn and quartered. 'Great persons by leave of the king may be beheaded.'

She completes her list of punishments with some account of the use of the stocks, the pillory, whipping at the cart's tail, branding in hand or cheek and transportation. The Marshalsea and Fleet prisons were mainly for debtors who, with their families, might well be there for life.

Finally she writes with great satisfaction : 'Here is noe wracks or tortures nor no slaves made, only such as are banish'd sometimes into our foreign plantations there to work.' Thus does each age pride itself on its humanity and wisdom in dealing with wrongdoers.

Celia Fiennes did not find corruption only in legal practice. Parliament, too, left much to be desired. King and people, as represented in the Commons, did not always honour each other as they should 'with a just and equal footing—but alas! it's too sadly to be bemoaned, the best and sweetest wine turns soonest sour, so we by folly, faction and wickedness have endeavour'd our own ruin and were it not for God's providentiall care and miraculous works we should at this day have been a people left to utter dispaire, having only the agraveteing thought of our once happy constitution to lament its loss the more'.

When her busy, cheerful life ended at the ripe age of 79 her body was, by her own wish, carried very quietly from her London houses to the churchyard at Newton Toney for burial beside her parents. There today can still be seen the simple inscription of her name and dates beneath those of her father. In her will she wrote that she had lost a good deal of land property; she had always given to charity and been generous to her relatives. But there was still a long list of gifts to relatives and friends—furniture, pictures, clothes and jewels. It is not known into whose hands her manuscripts first came but by good fortune they eventually saw the light.

Several male writers of the same period also travelled through England and recorded their findings—Daniel Defoe, Arthur Young, C. P. Moritz—yet the woman's viewpoint supplied by this vigorous, forthright observer has its own special charm. Many women travellers have written their stories since her day, and been deservedly praised. Celia Fiennes was the pioneer.

FIVE
Fanny Burney

FRANCES (FANNY) BURNEY was the first really famous English-woman novelist. She was blessed in her own nature and gifts, in her family and in her work. Born in 1752 in the reign of George II, she was the second daughter of Dr Charles Burney, the famous musician whose gifts as performer, teacher and writer graced the second half of the eighteenth century.

Among Burney's friends were Dr Samuel Johnson the great lexicographer, David Garrick the actor, Sir Joshua Reynolds the painter, and Oliver Goldsmith the novelist, poet and dramatist. Dr Burney was a good family man, his children met many such famous people in their own home and were encouraged to join in the social life around them.

Dr Burney's first wife was of Hugenot (French Protestant) descent, a cultured and gifted woman who taught her children to appreciate good reading, both English and French. Fanny was a very slow learner. Her younger sister could read long before she did, but her mother noticed that Fanny had a quick understanding and an amazing memory. When Mrs Burney died Fanny was only nine, and the little girl felt very deeply the loss of her mother. She had a warm, sensitive nature and was always devoted to her father and never so happy as when she was helping him in some way. But she was rather shy and quiet and it was not until she felt at ease with anyone that she found much to say.

Dr Burney used to say that from her eleventh birthday all his friends called her 'The Old Lady'. Little did they then realise that their looks, behaviour and words were all being noted in Fanny's

mind; almost without knowing it, 'the little old lady' was collecting material that would later be invaluable in her novel-writing.

Soon after her mother died she met someone whose influence on
her was almost as great as her father's. Twenty-five year old
Samuel Crisp became a close friend of Dr Burney and his family;
he was a bachelor with many interests, a musician and painter, and
a lively talker. He lived at Chessington in Surrey and came up to
London from time to time. He and nine-year old Fanny became
firm friends; he was soon 'Daddy Crisp', her confidant in many
matters, and he in turn described her later as 'Fannikin, the dearest
thing to me on earth'.

About twelve months after his wife's death, Dr Burney married
a second time. His new wife, whom he had known earlier in King's
Lynn where he had been an organist, was a widow with one
daughter, Maria Allen, who became Fanny's life-long friend. The
second Mrs Burney proved a good stepmother and a new family
life was begun.

Fanny never seems to have been to school, although there were
several good boarding schools for girls at the time. Education was
not compulsory in those days, and families had to make their own
arrangements. She and her sisters seem to have studied languages
and literature at home, together with music, as was to be expected.
Her sisters all played some instrument and sang, but Fanny preferred to be a listener. The eighteenth century was a great age of
opera (Mozart, Verdi), and as a family the Burneys were so
devoted to opera that the girls studied Italian so that they could
enjoy opera more. Not only did they regularly visit the Opera
House at Covent Garden, but they also stayed up at the supper
parties Dr Burney used to give for the principal singers.

This and much more information comes directly from Fanny
herself. Quite early on, she begun to 'scribble' stories which her
sister Susan much enjoyed. Mrs Burney, however, thought that
writing was unsuitable for girls, and a waste of valuable time. So
Fanny dutifully made a bonfire of all her early efforts. But a born
writer will always find an outlet, as Fanny soon discovered, although
she never thought at first of publishing anything. When she was
about sixteen she began to keep a diary, and continued to do so all
her life. This diary, published after her death, reveals a gay, amusing yet thoughtful young woman who later won the admiration of
many readers of her novels.

The Diary opens with an address to 'Nobody': 'To whom, then,
must I dedicate my wonderful, surprising and interesting Adven-

tures? To *whom* dare I reveal my private opinion of my nearest relations? My secret thoughts of my dearest friends, my own hopes, fears, reflections and dislikes? Nobody! To Nobody, then, will I write my Journal, since to Nobody can I be wholly unreserved—to Nobody can I reveal every thought, every wish of my heart, with the most unlimited confidence, the most unremitting sincerity to the end of my life.'

Fifty years later the author carefully went through everything she had written, but saw no reason to change anything. So the pages remain full of vivid portraits of people, famous and un-known, oddities often, for she loved the unusual, always presented in the glow of her own good humour and enlivened by her sense of fun.

The Fanny that most people knew was small and rather short-sighted, but she was attractive and kept her youthful looks long after she was mature. Her face used to reveal her feelings too easily for her own comfort. Her father said 'poor Fanny's face tells us what she thinks whether she will or no!'. To her Diary she once confided, 'Nobody, I believe, has so *very* little command of countenance as myself—I could feel my whole face on fire.'

Occasionally she showed her high spirits by doing 'my imita-tions' of various people—not as 'set pieces', but spontaneously to amuse herself and any member of her family who happened to be in the room. But it was in her Diary that she revealed herself most clearly : she might have been shy in company, but putting pen to paper in the privacy of her own room she often became as garrulous in writing as she was reserved in speech.

The early Diaries contain many notes of the books she read. She enjoyed translated versions of Greek and Roman poets, histories and the writings of her own time and of the earlier eighteenth century, especially the novels of Richardson and Fielding, the first real English novelists. She read Goldsmith's *The Vicar of Wakefield* shortly after it came out, while she was in her teens and praised it highly, although she was not satisfied until it had made her cry. Later she attended an early performance of *She Stoops to Conquer* and reported, 'Dr Goldsmith has just brought on the stage a new comedy called *She Stoops to Conquer* . . . it is very laughable and comic; but I know not how it is, almost all diversions are insipid at present, to me, except the opera'.

A few short extracts from the early diaries will illustrate her easy style. A visit to Gloucester : 'I saw enough of it to die contented if I never should see it again.' She could write crisply when she chose but it was usually about places—which interested her less than people. Her hosts in Gloucester were Dr and Mrs Wall who were decidedly eccentric, although very kind; Mrs Wall spent nearly all her time at her toilet, and Dr Wall played a variety of musical instruments, all very badly.

Fanny wrote : 'We found the Doctor playing upon the bassoon, and, as usual, surrounded with the Lord knows how many other instruments. He presently flung them all away—and what do you think for?—why to romp with me. I am sure you would never have guessed that; but the less he found me inclined to this sort of sport the more determined he seemed to pursue it and we danced round the room, hayed in and out with the chairs and all that, till it grew so late that he ordered dinner.' Dr Wall was the child, Fanny the adult.

A small party : 'When supper was over all who had voices worth hearing were made to sing—none shone more than Mr Adams; though in truth he has little or no voice yet he sung with so much taste and feeling that few very *fine* voices could give equal pleasure . . . Mr Robinson also sung and showed to advantage his fine teeth and face. Miss Dalrymple also showed to *dis*-advantage her conceit and self-approbation; Hetty, with *one* song only, gave more pleasure than any other . . . Poor Mrs Pringle, who hates music, . . . was on the rack of impatience and vexation all the time. She is seldom silent three minutes, yet seldom speaks without applause; therefore this musical entertainment was absolute torture to her. For the life of me I could not forbear laughing.'

Private theatricals at Mr Crisp's house at Chessington : Fanny describes some members of the party, 'Mademoiselle Rosat, . . . about forty, tall and elegant in person and dress, very sensible, extremely well-bred, and, when in spirits, droll and humourous. But she has been very unhappy and her misfortunes have left indelible traces on her mind, which subjects her to extreme low spirits. Yet I think her a great acquisition to Chessington. Miss Cooke, who, I believe, is forty too, but has so much good nature and love of mirth in her that she still appears a girl . . . Miss Barsarti . . . is extremely clever and entertaining, possesses amazing powers of mimicry, and an uncommon share of humour . . . Mr Featherstone—a middle-aged gentleman who, having broken his leg, walks upon crutches. He is equally ugly and cross.'

Fanny then describes how she and her step-sister Maria and Miss Barsarti, the actress, appeared before the company in some kind of play. She began rather badly herself by rushing off in a panic when the audience applauded her entrance. Maria appeared as a man, dressed in clothes borrowed from Mr Featherstone, apparently no longer cross. This ill-fitting costume, too broad in the back, too wide in the sleeves and too small in the wig, caused such an uproar that the play was held up, while 'horse laughs were echoed from side to side. Hetty was almost in convulsions, Mr Crisp hollowed, Mr Featherstone absolutely wept with excessive laughing and even Mamselle Rosat leaned her elbows on her lap and could not support herself upright. What rendered Maria's appearance more ridiculous was that, being wholly unused to acting, she forgot her audience and acted as often with her back to them as her face; and her back was really quite too absurd, the full breadth of her height.'

At a masquerade: 'Everybody was then unmasked and when I presently turned hastily round . . . what was my surprise at seeing the Dutchman! I had no idea that he was under fifty, when behold, he scarce looked three and twenty. I believe my surprise was very manifest for Mynheer could not forbear laughing. On his part he paid me many compliments, repeating and with much civility congratulating himself on his choice, "I have been smoaking them all round," cried he, for he had always a tobacco pipe in his hand, "till at last a happy whiff blew away your mask and fixed me so fortunately."

'Nothing could be more droll than the first dance we had after the unmasking; the pleasure which appeared in some countenances and the disappointment pictured in others made the most singular contrast imaginable, and to see the old turned young and the young old—in short, every face appeared different from what we expected. The Old Witch, in particular, we found, was a young officer. The Punch, who had made himself as broad as long, was a very young and handsome man; but what most surprised me was the Shepherd, whose own face was so stupid that we could *scarcely* tell whether he had taken off his mask or *not*!'

Some admirers: The young 'Dutchman' had evidently been charmed by Fanny, as he met her on several later occasions and tried hard to pursue her acquaintance. Fanny, however, was not seriously interested in him or indeed in any of the young men who sought her hand in marriage. Both her father and Mr Crisp were anxious that she should not miss a good offer but they realised they could never force her against her own judgment.

A Mr Barlow had for some time pestered her, refusing to be turned down. Fanny described the end of the affair: 'I rose and walked to the window, thinking it high time to end a conversation already much too long; and then he again began to entreat me not to be so *very severe*. I told him that I was *sure* I should never alter the answer I made at first; that I was very happy at home and not at all inclined to try my fate elsewhere. "I am extremely sorry to detain you so long, Ma'am," he said, in a melancholy voice. I made no answer. He then walked about the room; and then again besought my leave to ask me how I did some other time. I absolutely, though civilly, refused it and told him frankly that, fixed as I was, it was better that we should not meet. He then took his leave—returned back—took leave, and returned again.'

Finally he went and although Fanny was sorry for him, 'I could almost have *jumped* for joy when he was gone, to think the affair was finally over.'

Dr Burney was disappointed, as he felt it would have been a good match. But when he realised how miserable Fanny had been made by it, he was full of tenderness. ' "God knows," continued he, "I wish not to part with my girls, only, don't be too hasty." Thus relieved, restored to future hopes, I went to bed, light, happy and thankful, as if escaped from destruction.'

However, Mr Barlow paid her yet one more uncomfortable visit to ask about her health. Fanny was firm and polite. 'Sorry as I am for Mr B. who is a worthy young man, I cannot involve myself in a life of discomfort for his satisfaction.'

David Garrick and his wife were frequent and welcome visitors in the Burney household. Fanny writes rapturously of Garrick both as man and actor. Indeed, he captivated the whole family, just as he charmed his packed audiences at Drury Lane theatre.

'After tea we were cheered indeed; for *rap-tap-tap* and entered Mr and Mrs Garrick and their two nieces. Mr Garrick who has lately been very ill, is delightfully recovered, looks as handsome as ever I saw him.' Garrick had a habit of calling on Dr Burney at eight o'clock in the morning, to the horror of the girls, Hetty, Fanny and Susan. Their father's late-night concerts and parties usually ended so late that no one was up at that time of morning.

'Mr Garrick, to my great confusion, has again surprised the house before we were up; but really, my father keeps such late hours at night that I have no resolution to rise before eight in the morning. My father himself was only on the stairs when this early, industrious, active, charming man came. I dressed myself immediately, but found he was going as I entered the study. He stopped short, and, with his accustomed drollery exclaimed, "Why now, why are *you* come down now to keep me? But this will never do (looking at his watch). You will never marry at this rate—to keep such late hours! No, I shall keep all the young men from you." Later, as he was just going, he said with a very comical face, to me, "I like you! I like you all! I like your looks! I like your manner," and then, opening his arms with an air of heroics, he cried, "I am tempted to run away with you all, one after another." We all longed to say, "Pray do!"'

Garrick as actor is often mentioned, always with admiration. Of his *Richard the Third* she comments : 'Garrick was sublimely horrible. Good heavens, how he made me shudder whenever he appeared. It is inconceivable how terribly great he is in this character! I will never see him so disfigured again; he seemed so truly the monster he performed that I felt myself glow with indignation every time I saw him. The applause he met with exceeds all belief of the absent. I thought at the end they would have torn the house down; our seats shook under us.'

Her first meeting with the testy Dr Johnson is best recorded in a letter to Mr Crisp in 1777. Dr Burney gave regular Thursday morning parties at home and on this occasion Dr Johnson entered the room while Hetty and Susan Burney were singing a duet.

'He is indeed very ill-favoured; is tall and stout; but stoops terribly; he is almost bent double. His mouth is almost constantly opening and shutting as if he was chewing. He has a strange method of frequently twirling his fingers, and twisting his hands. His body is in continual agitation, see-sawing up and down; his feet are never a moment quiet, and, in short, his whole person is in *perpetual motion*. His dress, too, considering the times and that he had meant to put on *his best clothes*, being engaged to dine in a large company, was as much out of the common road as his figure; he had a large wig, snuff-coloured coat, and gold buttons, but no ruffles to his shirt, and black worsted stockings. He is shockingly near-sighted, and did not, until she held out her hand to him, even know Mrs Thrale. He poked his nose over the keys of the harp-sichord till the duet was finished and then my Father introduced Hetty to him as an old acquaintance and he cordially kissed her ...

'His attention, however, was not diverted five minutes from the books, as we were in the library; he pored over them, shelf by shelf, almost touching the backs of them with his eye-lashes, as he read their titles. At last having fixed upon one, he began, without further ceremony, to read (to himself) all the time standing at a distance from the company. We were all very much provoked, as we perfectly languished to hear him talk; but it seems he is the most silent creature, when not particularly drawn out, in the world . . .

'Chocolate being then brought, we adjourned to the dining-room. And here, Dr Johnson, being taken from the books, entered freely and most cleverly into conversation; though it is remarkable he never speaks at all but when spoken to; nor does he ever *start,* though he so admirably *supports* any subject.'

This letter and many others written to Mr Crisp and to her sisters and various friends show Fanny Burney to be as lively in correspondence as she was in her diary. Mr Crisp evidently enjoyed teasing her and challenging her opinions. He had said in one letter that men 'are just what they were designed to be—Animals of Prey—all men are cats, all young girls mice—morsels—dainty bits —such is human nature—the only security is flight, or Bars and Bolts and Walls'.

Fanny replied, 'Though I allow this to be very natural, I cannot forbear noticing that it seems of necessity for men to be capricious and fickle, even about trifles' and, pursuing the matter in another letter, she wrote, 'Coquetry, I must acknowledge, is almost universal but I know fewer girls exempt from that passion than from any other . . . I will therefore only say that though I readily allow you [men] a *general* superiority over us in most other particulars, yet in constancy, gratitude and virtue, I regard you as unworthy all competition or comparison. The flights and failings of women are oftener from some defect in the *head* than in the *heart*, which is just reversed by you—so that where we are *weak* you are *wicked*—now which is the least justifiable?'

To this broadside there seems to have been no reply.

But letters and her diary, parties, concerts and theatres, were only part of Fanny Burney's life. Her father was long engaged on writing his *History of Music*; a work which, published in 1775, became a standard authority on the subject. Fanny, acting as her father's secretary, had written out by hand every single word of it for the publisher. There were no typewriters in Fanny's day. She was thrilled by the many tributes that her father received on this great achievement.

Most important of all, however, was her own secret work, the writing of a long novel. This she did usually at night and, as she hoped to send it to the same publishers of her father's *History of Music,* she wrote it in 'a feigned hand,' lest anyone should recognise her writing and discover her to be the author.

66

At last, in January 1778, *Evelina, or A Young Lady's Entrance into the World* was ready, and with great excitement and fear Fanny entrusted it to one of her brothers to take to Lowndes the publisher, as from a 'Mr Grafton'. After enlarging the book by a third volume at the publisher's request, 'to be replete with modern characters' she was delighted to be paid £20 for it. At a later stage, when the book was a brilliant success, she received another £10. At first, no one except her brothers and sisters knew she was the author. She was so afraid that her father and stepmother would disapprove of the book, that she put off telling them as long as possible. But just before it was published she confided to her father that she had written something. It happened just as he was seeing her off on a visit to an uncle at Worcester:

'While I was taking leave I was so much penetrated by my dear Father's kind parting embrace that in the fullness of my heart I could not forbear telling him I had sent a manuscript to Mr Lowndes; earnestly, however, beseeching him never to divulge it, nor to demand a sight of such trash as I could scribble . . . He could not help laughing; but, I believe, was much surprised at the communication. He desired me to acquaint him from time to time how *my work* went on, called himself the *'Pere confident'* and kindly promised to guard my secret as cautiously as I could wish.'

But he did not recognise the book when he first saw it, although it was dedicated to him in verses which began:

> Oh, Author of my being!—far more dear
> To me than light, than nourishment or rest,

and ends

> Oh, of my life at once the source and joy!
> If e'er thy eyes these feeble lines survey,
> Let not their folly their intent destroy.
> Accept the tribute—but forget the lay.

The book's first appearance is announced in Fanny's Diary: 'This year was ushered in by a grand and most important event— for at the latter end of January the literary world was favoured with the first publication of the ingenious, learned and most profound Fanny Burney!—I doubt not but this memorable affair will, in future times, mark the period whence chronologers will date the zenith of the polite arts in this island. This elaborate authoress has named her most elaborate performance, *Evelina, or A Young*

Lady's Entrance into the World. Perhaps this may seem a rather bold attempt and title for a female whose knowledge of the world is very confined, and whose inclinations as well as situation incline her to a private and domestic life. All I can urge is that I have presumed to trace the accidents and adventures to which a "young woman" is liable. I have not pretended to shew the world what it actually *is* but what it *appears* to a girl of seventeen—and, so far as that, surely any girl who is *past* seventeen, may safely do.'

The self-mockery of the first part is characteristic of many entries in the diary, but her modesty also appears when she wrote. 'I thought *Evelina*'s only admirers would be schoolgirls and destined her to no nobler a habitation than a circulating library.'

This comment is interesting since the libraries were at that time the purveyors of third-rate stories of the kind deplored by Sir Anthony Absolute in Sheridan's play, *The Rivals*—'a circulating library is an evergreen tree of diabolical knowledge'. One of the reasons for *Evelina*'s success was the dearth of good writing that had followed the grand days of Richardson and Fielding earlier in the century. The same public which had recently welcomed the wholesome vigour of *She Stoops to Conquer* and the gentle romance of *The Vicar of Wakefield* was ready to acclaim the adventures of the ingenuous and beautiful *Evelina*.

When Fanny went to buy a copy of the book from Lowndes, who was bookseller as well as publisher, she was assured by him that the unknown gentleman who wrote it was 'a master of his subject and well-versed in the manners of the times'. Much gratified she departed, leaving him still in ignorance. Soon she was able to write of the book's success in the libraries: 'every butcher and baker, cobbler and tinker, throughout the three kingdoms, might now see it for the small tribute of threepence.'

Into *Evelina* had gone all the knowledge and experience of the social world that the author possessed. The theme of the novel was simply the adventures of a young girl 'of virtuous mind, a good understanding and a feeling heart'. She had been brought up in complete seclusion until the age of seventeen and it was her ignorance of all the ways of the world outside her small country home that led to experiences pleasant and painful in the maze of high life and low life in London and Bath. The author's avowed intention was 'to draw characters from Nature, though not from life and to mark the manners of the times'. This she faithfully accomplished; aristocrats—the noble and the dastardly; townspeople—the worthy and the vulgar; the whole bustling scene of London life is peopled by amazingly well-contrasted characters.

To highlight these contrasts, Fanny gives her motherless heroine a wealthy and aristocratic father whom she had never met and a plebeian grandmother of equal wealth and completely vulgar associations. These and the other characters, including the abnormally virtuous and charming nobleman whom she eventually marries, are seen through the eyes of Evelina as she unfolds her story in letters to the saintly man who was her guardian. It was natural that Fanny Burney, the accomplished letter-writer, should choose to use this letter method. This had been done already with great success by Samuel Richardson, one of the earliest novelists, in *Clarissa*.

When at last Dr Burney *did* read the book, Fanny was staying at Chessington, recovering from an illness. Her sister Susan wrote to tell her what had happened :

' "Why, Susan," said he to me, "I have got Fan's book." '

' "Lord, sir, have you?" '

' "Yes, but I suppose you must not tell her. Poor Fan's *such* a prude." '

' "Oh, I don't know, sir; she knows *you* know of it—'tis only others." '

' "Oh," said he quick, "I shall keep it lodged in my *sanctum sanctorum*. I would not betray the poor girl for the world. But upon my soul, I like it vastly. Do you know, I began to read it with Lady Hales and Miss Coussmaker yesterday." '

' "Lord," cried I, a little alarmed, "you did not tell them—" '

' "Tell them? no, certainly; I said 'twas a book had been recommended to me—they'll never know, and they like it *vastly*, but upon my soul, there's something in the preface and dedication *vastly strong and well-written*—better than I could have expected—and yet I did not think it would be *trash* when I began it ... the girl's account of public places is very animated and natural and not *common*—it really appears to me that Lowndes has a *devilish good bargain* of it, for the book will *sell*—it has real merit and the *Review* alone would sell it." '

A little later, Dr Burney read it aloud to his wife, without naming the author and she was full of praise and later of delight when she learned of Fanny's success.

Meantime everyone of importance was reading the new novel. Edmund Burke, Sir Joshua Reynolds and Edward Gibbon, who read the book in one day, were loud in its praises. The fashionable

Mrs Thrale said, 'There's a great deal of human *life* in this book and of the manners of the present time. It's writ by somebody that knows the *top* and the *bottom*, the *highest* and *lowest* of mankind. It's very good language, and there's an infinite deal of fun in it.' She introduced it to Dr Johnson who praised it so highly as actually to compare it with the novels of Richardson and Fielding. This was Fanny's greatest moment for he still did not know who had written the book.

She wrote, 'Dr Johnson's approbation!—it almost crazed me with agreeable surprise—it gave me such a flight of spirits that I danced a jig to Mr Crisp, without any preparation, music or explanation, to his no small amazement and diversion.'

The devoted Susan wrote, 'I had thought before that you had reached *the summit of grandeur* in Mrs Thrale's, Mrs Cholmondley's and my Father's warm approbation; but *Johnsons's* raises you so many degrees higher, that you now *certainly* rest secure on your literary throne, for no one can ever change it.'

But the days of her anonymity were over and Fanny had to learn to receive homage. Mrs Thrale gave a luncheon in her honour where Dr Johnson assured her it was a great privilege to be seated beside her. She was encouraged to write again and in 1782 her second novel *Cecilia* was published. For this she received £250 and the publisher dared to print two thousand copies instead of the usual five hundred, so great was her fame.

One lady wrote, '*Cecilia* sends us into people's houses with our eyes swelled out of our heads with weeping. We take the book into the carriage and weep . . . The children wept and sobbed aloud; my heart was bursting with agony, and we all seemed in despair.'

Evidently pathos was popular in fashionable society then. An interesting point about the unhappy course of Cecilia's love affairs was that Fanny Burney, as author, commented that her troubles were due to 'pride and prejudice'. A young reader, herself already a writer, noted the phrase and its application by Miss Burney, whose work she admired. Some years later it took on a new significance when Jane Austen used it as the title and theme of her own very different novel.

Although *Evelina* had evoked much laughter, there had been pathetic passages over which readers had enjoyed a good cry. Modern readers will be likely to read both books dry-eyed; it is unlikely, however, that many people today enjoy *Cecilia*; it is very long and lacks the freshness and variety which makes *Evelina* good reading still. Fanny Burney was not an inventive writer; she was an observer of the contemporary scene and she never repeated the success of *Evelina*, although she continued to write for some years.

Among the scores of well-known people who congratulated Fanny on her novel was King George III. This happened in 1785 when she was visiting her friend at Windsor, Mrs Delany, a great friend of the Royal family.

The King entered, unannounced, the room where Fanny was in the midst of a game with a small girl and two other adults. To her horror she could not escape as the King was standing in the one doorway.

He greeted Mrs Delany and then asked her in a loud whisper, 'Is that Miss Burney?' and on her answering, 'Yes, sir,' he bowed and with a countenance of the most perfect good humour, came close up to me. A most profound reverence on my part arrested the progress of my intended retreat.

'Later he saw on the table a book of drawings and turning over the leaves he said, "Pray, does Miss Burney draw too?" "I believe not, sir," answered Mrs D., "at least she does not tell." "Oh!" cried he, laughing, "that's nothing, she is not apt to tell. She never does, you know! Her father told me that himself. He told me the whole history of her *Evelina*. And I shall never forget his face when he spoke of his feelings at first taking up the book—he looked quite frightened, just as if he was doing it at that moment."

'Then, coming up close to me, he said, "But what? What? How was it?" "Sir," cried I, not well understanding him. "How came you—how happened it? What? What?" "I—I only wrote, sir, for my own amusement—only in some odd, idle hours." "But your publishing—your printing—how was that?" "That was only, sir, because—" I hesitated most abominably, not knowing how to tell him a long story, and growing terribly confused at these questions. The *what* was then repeated with so earnest a look that, forced to say something, I stammeringly answered—"I thought—sir—it would look very well in print."

'I do really flatter myself this is the silliest speech I ever made. I am quite provoked with myself for it; but a fear of laughing made me eager to utter anything, and by no means conscious, till I had spoken, of what I was saying. He laughed very heartily himself—well he might—and walked away to enjoy it, crying out, "Very fair indeed! that's being very fair and honest." '

The following year, 1786, through the influence of Mrs Delany Fanny Burney was appointed Assistant Keeper of the Robes to

Queen Charlotte, a post she held until 1791 when ill health obliged her to resign. Her Diary tells of her experiences at Court and the Queen's kindness to her. This, however, sometimes made things unpleasant because of the jealousy of the Chief Keeper of the Robes, a German lady of uncertain temper.

But Fanny enjoyed the life at Court, particularly when she was not on duty and could read and continue her writing of *Camilla*, her latest novel. Her duties called for early rising; she was required to dress the Queen at 7.30 each morning; another lady handed the various garments to Fanny, who did the actual dressing, which included adjusting the fashionable hoop and handing the inevitable fan. That over, she was free until a quarter to twelve, except on Wednesdays and Saturdays, when she was needed an hour earlier for 'curling and craping the hair' before the grand toilette of the day. Nothing more was then expected of her until the end of the day unless there were balls or other Court functions.

Her Diary chronicles many interesting events, one being the attempted murder of the King by a mad woman in London. She wrote of his calm kindliness as he reassured the people he was unhurt and gave orders that the woman was to be gently treated. In 1788 she sadly recorded the first bout of mental illness of the King and the great distress of the Queen.

The following year he had made a temporary recovery and the whole Court went by road in easy stages to Weymouth. Fanny was delighted that everywhere along their journey the King was hailed by crowds who cheered and sang their joy at his recovery. When, after nearly a week's travel, they reached Gloucester Lodge, Weymouth, 'the whole town and Melcomb Regis and half the country of Dorset seemed assembled to welcome their Majesties'. The King improved daily and even went sea-bathing, while in a nearby 'bathing machine' a band of fiddlers burst into *God save the King* as His Majesty left his machine and plunged into the water.

Fanny flung herself into all the joys and sorrows of the Royal family but her own health suffered and she had, at last, to beg the Queen to let her retire. The Queen asked her to stay with her as long as possible and she remained for another six months, until 1791. The royal pair gave her a present of one hundred guineas and grieved much at her going. Later the Queen, in conversation with a friend, said of her,

'Oh, as to character, she is what we call in German, "true as gold", and in point of heart there is not, all the world over, one better.' Three years after her leaving Court, the novel *Camilla* appeared, dedicated by Royal permission to the Queen herself.

Two years later, in 1793, Fanny Burney married a French Army officer, an emigré from the Revolution, General D'Arblay. The marriage was a happy one, as Fanny's letters to her sister, Susan, plainly show. With her husband and young son she went to France in 1802 and lived there for some years, during Napoleon's rise to power. In 1814–15 they were in Brussels in the stirring time of the battle of Waterloo but they returned to England almost immediately after this and settled down to a peaceful life. Fanny outlived both her husband and son. In fact she did not die until 1840, at the grand age of eighty-eight.

Fanny Burney's great achievement was *Evelina,* which made history as the earliest major novel by a woman writer. It remains in circulation today because it paints a vivid and accurate picture of the social life of the later eighteenth century. No quotations from the book are made because short passages would not do justice to the complicated events of the story. Fanny's style has already been illustrated by the quotations from her Diary : the novel is written in the same easy, conversational manner. It must always be remembered that people and events are pictured as they were seen through the eyes of a very young, inexperienced girl. *Evelina* is a 'must' for all lovers of a genuine period piece.

SIX

Jane Austen

LIKE HER CONTEMPORARY, Fanny Burney (her senior by some ten years) Jane Austen was a member of a large, devoted and happy family. But while Fanny Burney, from her earliest childhood, enjoyed the literary and artistic life of London, Jane Austen spent her forty-one years of life almost entirely in the quiet surroundings of the Hampshire countryside.

Jane was the youngest but one of a family of seven—five boys and two girls—of the Reverend George Austin, rector of Steventon, and his wife Cassandra. From both parents the family inherited an all-round culture that gave the sons a good start in the world—James became a clergyman and later followed in his father's footsteps at Steventon; Edward, after managing the estate of a wealthy friend became his heir; Henry was a banker in London and the two others went to sea, one becoming an Admiral, the other a Vice-Admiral.

All the brothers married, some more than once. Their numerous families were an increasing interest to Jane and her elder sister Cassandra. They both lived at home and led busy lives, as their mother was often ill and much had to be done about the house and garden. The two girls were close companions and their mother once remarked, 'If Cassandra were going to have her head cut off, Jane would insist on sharing her fate.'

For the first twenty-five years of her life (1775–1801) Jane Austen lived quietly at Steventon in the closely knit community of friends and neighbours. It was from her observation of these people and activities that she knew so intimately that the material for her novels was accumulated. Yet she did not reproduce living persons in her books. She said that she thought it quite fair to note any peculiarities and weaknesses she saw, but her aim was to create—not to reproduce. Her 'creations' became lifelike individuals—the kind of people whom everyone has met at some time or would like to meet.

Jane began, again like Fanny Burney whose work she greatly admired, by writing to amuse herself and her family. When she was fourteen she had written a series of burlesques, wildly exaggerated mockeries of the many feeble novels that had appeared in imitation of the 'Gothic' novels of Mrs Ann Radcliffe. These thrillers were in great demand in the circulating libraries of the day and because she enjoyed novels so much Jane had evidently read some of them.

She had real respect for Mrs Radcliffe's writing and recognised the place of the horror-novel in literature. But her sense of the ridiculous—never very far away in all her writing—could only laugh at the absurdity of such works as *Mysterious Warnings, The Necromancer of the Black Forest* or *Horrid Mysteries.* So her *Effusions of Fancy,* as the burlesques were called, were satirical and absurd and the characters mere puppets.

Her famous novels are very different. They deal with people and situations belonging to the world of everyday life. Nothing supernatural happens, no life-and-death struggles are waged, no melodrama is presented. Yet in these domestic tales the author's wit shines on the characters and sparkles so much that the pleasant people are made more delightful, the unpleasant made to look foolish, and the bores are comic.

She is a 'timeless' writer. The human, domestic problems that she deals with are familiar to every generation. Her special quality among women writers is that she sees right into the foibles and follies of human nature and finds them not irritating or forbidding but more often amusing and even endearing.

Jane is not much interested in moral issues—the depths are not her province. But behaviour and manners and moods are constantly revealed for the reader's delight. This accords with her own nature. She was affectionate but reserved, temperate in all her emotions, capable of great love but completely unsentimental. Above all, she was quick to see and enjoy life's absurdities.

She never dealt, either in her books or her personal letters, with ideas and events beyond her own sphere. Even though her sailor brothers risked their lives in the sea warfare raging between the English and the French Navies, and even though invasion of England by Napoleon was a very real threat, she hardly mentioned such things. She concentrated on what was near at hand.

The result is six novels, perfect of their kind. Jane was a perfectionist. She revised and rewrote until she was satisfied she could make no further improvement. She herself likened her novel-writing to painting miniatures on ivory with a very fine brush. There was a firm delicacy about all she did. Her handwriting was small and clear, her needlework exquisite. Similarly, her treatment of people—whether in real life or in her books—was deft and sure. She could and did comfort the unhappy, as her relatives testified, and she was a capable and patient nurse on many occasions. Through all the commonplace events of life her sense of fun enlivened the scene but, like her heroine Elizabeth Bennet, she did *not* play with serious matters nor ridicule individuals. Her censure was reserved for selfishness and snobbery, as is seen in all the novels.

To the pretentious characters she was merciless—Lady Catherine de Bourgh is a monument of unpleasantness, and her toady, the Rector, Mr Collins, has no redeeming feature in his colossal self-satisfaction. Yet laughter, and not disgust, is aroused in the reader (*Pride and Prejudice*). In *Emma* she shows how, by careful selection and a perfect sense of timing, she can make complete bores seem comic. The fussy valetudinarian Mr Woodhouse and the garrulous, good natured Miss Bates, might prove tiresome in real life but in Jane Austen's hands they are amusing and likeable because we are not allowed to see much of them at a time.

This kindliness tempered the sharpness of her irony in real life, too. In a letter to Cassandra, away on holiday, she wrote of the visit of a family friend who had often tried their patience : 'Poor Mrs Stent! it has been her lot to be always in the way; but we must be merciful, for perhaps in time we may come to be Mrs Stents ourselves, unequal to anything, and unwelcome to everybody.'

Jane Austen, as a writer, could certainly claim, like Alexander Pope, that her aim was to :

> Eye Nature's walk, shoot Folly as it flies,
> And catch the manners living as they rise.

But it was not the satirical Pope who was her favourite poet but the gentle Cowper and the rugged Crabbe.

She believed in happy endings for her stories, and said so in

Mansfield Park: 'Let other persons dwell on guilt and misery. I quit such odious subjects as soon as I can, impatient to restore everybody, not greatly in fault themselves, to tolerable comfort, and to have done with all the rest.'

She was the most unpretentious writer and did her work among the activities of the family sitting-room. She wrote on small sheets of paper which were at once put aside if she was called to the kitchen or garden. She knew no other writers personally and had no encouragement from outside her own circle. Her success, when it came, was modest and took her completely by surprise. But her reputation has grown with the years and today if a writer's work is described as having 'a touch of Jane' it is quite a compliment.

Quiet as it was, Jane Austen's life falls into three distinct sections; the first was at Steventon where her family lived from 1775–1801. As she grew up Jane enjoyed the social life of the district. She liked walking, exchanging visits—she sometimes visited some cousins in Bath—and dancing at the balls given in different country houses. Smaller parties and musical evenings were also held, all of which are mentioned in the novels.

Between 1795 and 1798 she had written the first versions of three novels—*Pride and Prejudice, Sense and Sensibility* and *Northanger Abbey.*

Her first novel *Pride and Prejudice* was originally to be called *First Impressions,* but, thanks to her favourite author, Fanny Burney, the title was changed. Miss Burney, in her novel *Cecilia,* had stated that Cecilia's unhappiness in love was 'the result of Pride and Prejudice'. Jane Austen recognised how aptly the phrase applied to her own hero and heroine. Cecilia however was an unhappy victim, but for the delightful Elizabeth Bennet there was happiness when the stubborn pride and snobbish prejudices of her suitor, Darcy, were overcome by his love and natural kindness.

Sense and Sensibility—at first named *Elinor and Marianne*—was originally written as a series of letters and it is interesting to see that in all the novels letters have a definite place and purpose. These are not only essential to the theme of the stories, but are used as a way of portraying the character of their writers.

The novel *Northanger Abbey* was written in gentle mockery of the fashionable sinister novels of the 'Gothic' school. It is set partly in Bath, where the writer's knowledge of its streets, assembly rooms and fashionable places is drawn upon. None of these novels, however, was published until some years later. There followed a long period when Jane Austen wrote nothing new.

The second phase of her life is during the years 1801–11 when the family lived in Bath. In 1801, her father decided to retire and move the household to Bath. This was not liked at first by his daughters, but when they had settled down they enjoyed the change.

At this time probably occurred the little-known romantic event of Jane Austen's life. Even her nephew, J. E. Austen-Leigh, who wrote a *Memoir* of her life, had to admit that there was 'one passage of romance in her history with which I am imperfectly acquainted, and to which I am unable to assign name, date, or place, though I have it on a sufficient authority.' That authority was Cassandra, who referred to the episode many years after Jane's death. It was also known to one of Jane's nieces who mentioned it to a group of friends. All that is definitely known is that Jane, who had taken almost no interest in earlier suitors, fell in love while on holiday with a naval officer. He proposed marriage and all seemed set fair for their happiness. But tragically, the young officer had a sudden attack of brain fever and died, having sent a last message to Jane.

Jane never referred to the affair, but in her last novel, *Persuasion*, published after her death, the character of the young naval officer, Captain Wentworth, is drawn so tenderly that there can be little doubt it was a portrait of her own lover.

While they lived in Bath she completed *Northanger Abbey* and in 1803 offered it to a Bath bookseller. He bought it for £10 but did nothing about publishing it. Thirteen years later her brother Henry bought it back again for £10, but by then Jane was not well enough to bring it up to date. However, in the preface she explained that some of the ideas and customs she had used were no longer fashionable and that in particular, tastes in popular reading had changed. The novel was eventually published, together with her last complete work, *Persuasion*, after her death in 1817.

In 1804 Mr Austen died. After living for a short time in Southampton, Mrs Austen and her daughters were invited by her wealthy son Edward to live in a house he owned at Chawton, close to his own estate. This proved an ideal arrangement and in these pleasant surroundings, which were the background to the last phase of her life, Jane Austen wrote her other novels from 1808–17.

Until 1811 none of her work had been published, but in that year *Sense and Sensibility* was published at her own expense. It was said to be 'By a Lady' and Jane had no hope of much success. However, it was well received, although no one knew who the author was. This success encouraged her, and when she was later paid £150 for it she was amazed, and thought it 'a prodigious recompense for that which has cost me nothing'.

Mansfield Park followed in 1812 and in 1813 *Pride and Prejudice* was published, fifteen years after she had first completed it. She was specially fond of its heroine, Elizabeth Bennet and wrote, 'I must confess I think her as delightful a creature as ever appeared in print, and how I shall be able to tolerate those who do not like *her*, at least, I do not know.' Fortunately nearly every reader of the book agrees with Elizabeth's creator.

Meanwhile she was not only busy writing *Emma*, but found time to visit London on several occasions to stay with her brother Henry, and go sight-seeing and on theatre jaunts with her favourite niece Fanny.

In 1815 she spent some months in London nursing Henry through a long and dangerous illness. His doctor, on hearing her name, which by that time was becoming talked about, told her that the Prince Regent, who was also his patient, liked her novels. He asked if the Prince's librarian, Mr Clarke, might visit her. This he did and was eager that she should write something specially for the Prince Regent and so enhance her reputation. He suggested a 'historical romance about the house of Cobourg (the royal house)—it would be a subtle compliment to Royalty'.

Jane, however, had to confess : 'I am fully sensible that a historical romance, founded on the House of Cobourg, might be much more to the purpose of profit or popularity than such pictures of domestic life in country villages as I deal in. But I could no more write a romance than an epic poem. I could not sit seriously down to write a serious romance under any other motive than to save my life; and if it were indispensable for me to keep it up and never relax into laughing at myself or at other people I am sure I should be hung before I had finished the first chapter. I must keep to my own style and go on in my own way; and though I may never succeed again in that, I am convinced that I should totally fail in any other.'

Mr Clarke was disappointed, but he admired her work and even persuaded the Prince Regent to accept the dedication of *Emma* to himself. When the Prince received his free copy from the publishers he wrote a letter to Jane thanking her for the 'very handsome book' (which, said Jane, suggested that he was at least pleased with the publisher's effort, if not with her own).

This was the last book published in her lifetime. She had never been strong and her health was already making her family anxious. She persevered with *Persuasion*, sometimes disappointing herself because she was too ill to write as she wished, and re-writing what dissatisfied her when she felt stronger. It was finished just before she went with Cassandra to stay in Winchester—only a few miles away—where the best doctors were. But she grew steadily worse, suffering what was then known as 'a decline', and died in 1817. She was forty-two.

She was buried in Winchester Cathedral where her grave is visited by admirers of her work from all over the world.

At the time of her death Cassandra wrote to their niece, Fanny: 'I have lost a treasure; such a sister, such a friend as can never have been surpassed. She was the sun of my life, the gilder of every pleasure, the soother of every sorrow, I had not a thought concealed from her, and it is as if I had lost a part of myself.'

This was not a tribute to the novelist but a lament for the beloved sister she was to survive for twenty-eight years. As Jane's reputation grew and her biography was requested, Cassandra, always reticent, destroyed all the intimate letters that her sister had written. Many other letters survive, but they deal with minor matters, showing the little things in which Jane found amusement and fun.

Jane Austen loved her nephews and nieces, and was very sympathetic toward their love-affairs on which her advice was sought several times. Her niece Fanny once confessed that she felt nothing at all for the eligible bachelor who wanted to marry her. Aunt Jane urged, 'Do not be in a hurry; the right man will come at last; you will, in the course of the next two or three years, meet with somebody more generally unexceptionable than anyone you have yet known, who will so completely attract you that you will feel you never really loved before.' And Fanny did eventually marry—a widower with six children! She herself had a large family and died in her ninetieth year. It was her eldest son, Lord Brabourne, who edited the published letters of Jane Austen.

Why are Jane's novels still so popular? Their style is unique and people have found it almost impossible to reproduce, abridge or even to adapt her stories. While it is true that versions recently made for stage, screen and television have been popular, the real quality of the novels is missing. The shafts of irony, the delicate hints of the author's own amused opinions of her characters, are lost in the change of medium.

Each novel has an identity and atmosphere entirely its own, yet all have one thing in common—the question of marriage, on which the whole action swings. In Jane Austen's day all parents were anxious that their daughters should make *suitable* marriages, but Jane Austen's heroines are remarkable in marrying for love. If fortune came along with love, so much the better. But fortune alone did not appeal to them. A contrast to the usual attitude of parents is stated in the opening sentence of *Pride and Prejudice* : 'It is a truth universally acknowledged that a single man in possession of a good fortune must be in want of a wife.'

Marriage is seen as an urgent necessity by Jane's worldly-minded characters, as well as the foolish ones, like Mrs Bennet and her empty-headed daughters Kitty and Lydia. Mrs Bennet was even ready to encourage the proposal of the pompous, incurably stupid clergyman, Mr Collins, to her high-spirited daughter Elizabeth. Elizabeth promptly refused him.

Mrs Bennet called to her husband : 'Oh, Mr Bennet, you are wanted immediately; we are all in an uproar. You must come and make Lizzie marry Mr Collins, for she vows she will not have him; and if you do not make haste he will change his mind and not have her.'

Mr Bennet arriving on the scene asks Elizabeth if she has indeed turned down Mr Collins' proposal. She assures him she has done so and her mother shouts that if she persists in her refusal, she will never talk to her daughter again. Mr Bennet comments, 'An unhappy alternative is before you, Elizabeth. From this day you must be a stranger to one of your parents. Your mother will never see you again if you do not marry Mr Collins, and I will never see you again if you do.'

When at last Elizabeth, after many doubts and difficulties becomes engaged to the wealthy Fitzwilliam Darcy, poor Mrs Bennet, who had always feared and disliked him, is beside herself with delight :

'Good gracious! Lord bless me! only think! dear me! Mr Darcy! who would have thought it? and is it really true? Oh, my sweetest Lizzie! How rich and how great you will be! what pin-money, what jewels, what carriages you will have! Jane's is nothing to it—nothing at all. I am so pleased, so happy! Such a charming man!—so handsome!—so tall! Oh, my dear Lizzie! pray apologise for my having disliked him so much before. I hope he will overlook it. Dear, dear Lizzie! A house in town! Everything that is charming! Three daughters married! Ten thousand a year! Oh, Lord! What will become of me. I shall go distracted.'

From this there was no doubt about her giving consent; and Elizabeth, rejoicing that such an outburst was heard only by herself, soon went away. But before she had been three minutes in her own room, her mother followed her.

'My dearest child,' she cried, 'I can think of nothing else! Ten thousand a year and very likely more! 'Tis as good as a lord! . . . But, my dearest love, tell me what dish Mr Darcy is particularly fond of, that I may have it tomorrow.'

This was a sad omen of what her mother's behaviour to Darcy himself might be, but the next day turned out much better than Elizabeth had dared to expect.

In contrast with Mrs Bennet's foolish delight is the cold, conventional attitude of John Dashwood in *Sense and Sensibility*. Dashwood noticed that a certain Colonel Brandon seemed to admire his sister Elinor :

'Who is this Colonel Brandon? Is he a man of fortune?'

'Yes, he has very good property in Dorsetshire.'

'I am glad of it. He seems a most gentlemanlike man; and, I think, Elinor, I may congratulate you on the prospect of a very respectable establishment in life.'

'Me, brother? What do you mean?'

'He likes you. I observed him narrowly and am convinced of it. What is the amount of his fortune?'

'I believe about two thousand a year.'

'Two thousand a year!' Then, working himself up to a pitch of enthusiastic generosity, he added, 'Elinor, I wish with all my heart it were twice as much for your sake.'

'Indeed, I believe you,' replied Elinor, 'but I am very sure that Colonel Brandon has not the smallest wish of marrying me.'

'You are mistaken, Elinor; you are very much mistaken. A very little trouble on your side secures him. Perhaps just at present he may be undecided; the smallness of your fortune may make him hang back; his friends may all advise him against it. But some of those little attentions and encouragements which ladies can so easily give will fix him in spite of himself. And there can be no reason why you should not try for him . . . Colonel Brandon must be the man; and no civility shall be wanting on my part to make him pleased with you and your family. It is a match that must give universal satisfaction.'

Fortunately, Elinor, who represents the 'Sense' of the novel's title, did not have to ensnare the Colonel, and was able to marry for love after all.

Fanny Price, the heroine of *Mansfield Park*, first appears as a timid, frightened child thrust into the opulent home of her aunt Lady Bertram, in sudden contrast to the crowded, rather squalid surroundings she had known before. At Mansfield Park she gradually makes a place for herself over the years. She is one of the characters who grows and blossoms but remains essentially self-effacing. Neither she nor her cousin, Edmund, whom she loved, are as interesting as other characters in the novel—the charming, clever and heartless brother and sister, Henry and Mary Crawford and the self-important and acquisitive Mrs Norris.

But Jane Austen makes sure that Fanny has her chance of married happiness, come what may. 'Scarcely had he [Edmund] done regretting Mary Crawford, and observing to Fanny how impossible it was that he should ever meet with such another woman, before it began to strike him whether a very different kind of woman might not do just as well—or a good deal better; whether Fanny herself was not growing as dear, as important to him, in all her smiles and all her ways, as Mary Crawford had ever been, and whether it might not be a possible, hopeful undertaking to persuade her that her warm and sisterly regard for him would be foundation enough for wedded love.

'I purposely abstain from dates on this occasion, that every one may be at liberty to fix their own, aware that the cure of unconquerable passions and the transfer of unchanging attachments must vary much as to time in different people. I only entreat everybody to believe that exactly at the time when it was quite natural that it should be so, and not a week earlier, Edmund did cease to care about Miss Crawford, and became as anxious to marry Fanny as Fanny herself could desire.'

Before writing *Emma*, Jane Austen told her sister, 'I am going to draw a heroine whom no one but myself will much like.' She was wrong, but it is easy to see what she meant. The opening sentence of the novel is characteristically clear and decisive :

'Emma Woodhouse, handsome, clever and rich, with a comfortable home and a happy disposition, seemed to unite some of the best blessings of existence; and had lived nearly twenty-one years in the world with very little to distress or vex her.'

But, unfortunately both for herself and others, Emma felt called to play Providence to her protégé, Harriet. In her efforts to bring about her marriage to the new clergyman Emma almost wrecked the perfectly suitable and happy attachment between Harriet and a local farmer. She also found that the clergyman's hopes were centred on herself—an unwelcome situation.

She struggled on from one mistake to another, always self-confident, always full of the best intentions and gradually, very gradually, learning something from them. Having imagined herself in love with the attractive but enigmatic Frank Churchill, she was very disappointed to learn of his fondness for someone else. But, as her various plans failed, she slowly began to notice the man who had always been part of her background, the one person who could, and did, rebuke her self-will and could always be relied upon to give good if unwelcome advice. Mr Knightly, her neighbour and friend, had always been taken for granted. Emma was aghast when she learned that Harriet believed him to be in love with herself because he had been kind to her in a time of difficulty. 'It darted through her with the speed of an arrow, that Mr Knightly must marry no one but herself!' As he had already decided that for himself, the future was indeed promising and, as usual, everything turned out well in the end.

Anne Elliot, the heroine of *Persuasion,* is perhaps the most thoughtful of Jane Austen's characters. Like Emma, she was motherless, but Anne's early years were made unhappy by the unpleasant attitude of her father and eldest sister.

'Vanity was the beginning and the end of Sir Walter Elliot's character—vanity of person and of situation. He had been remarkably handsome in his youth, and, at fifty-four, was still a very fine man. Few women could think more of their personal appearance than he did, nor could the valet of any new-made lord be more delighted with the place he held in society. He considered the blessing of beauty as inferior only to the blessing of a baronetcy; and the Sir Walter Elliot who united these gifts was the constant object of his warmest respect and devotion.'

To the snobbery of Sir Walter and his daughter, Elizabeth, Anne fell a victim, for she loved and was loved by a young naval officer, Captain Frederick Wentworth. But he had no fortune and even her old friend Lady Russell agreed with Sir Walter that this lively, impecunious young man was too dangerous a suitor for the nineteen-year-old Anne. It was Lady Russell's anxious warnings that at last persuaded Anne to put an end to the engagement, it was not fair even to him, she was told. So, despite arguments and pleas, she reluctantly agreed and her lover, feeling ill-used and miserable, left the country.

For seven years Anne remained constant to his memory, refusing

other good offers of marriage. She heard that his high hopes had
been fulfilled, he had risen in his profession and, since he had,
according to the newspapers, captured a number of enemy ships
he was probably a wealthy man.

Then, by a chain of circumstances, Captain Wentworth came
into her circle again but neither appeared anxious for more than
the most superficial exchanges. But their paths crossed constantly,
there were further encounters in Bath, there were misunderstand-
ings and suspicions until, at last, an all-important letter was written
and received. Part of it ran :

'I am half agony, half hope. Tell me not that I am too late,
that such precious feelings are gone for ever. I offer myself to you
with a heart even more your own than when you almost broke it,
eight years and a half ago ... I have loved none but you. Unjust
I may have been, weak and resentful I have been, but never in-
constant. You alone have brought me to Bath. For you alone I
think and plan. Have you not seen this? Can you fail to have
understood my wishes? I had not waited even these ten days,
could I have read your feelings, as I think you must have penetrated mine ... I must go uncertain of my fate; but I shall return
hither, or follow your party as soon as possible. A word, a look,
will be enough to decide whether I enter your father's house this
evening, or never.'

This letter was actually written in the room where Anne was
talking to a friend and fellow officer of Wentworth. He put it in
front of her as he went out of the room, and Anne's happiness
began the moment she opened it.

Persuasion introduces several naval men of different types and
Jane Austen is thoroughly at ease with these characters and sure
of all the necessary naval particulars; having two brothers who had
risen to high naval rank undoubtedly helped. If it seems odd that
men became rich by gaining prize-money for captured vessels it
was evidently the custom, as Jane herself wrote of her brother
Charles's prize-money. He had spent some of it on one occasion
buying gold chains and topaz crosses to send to his two sisters. Such
first-hand experience of sailors, both the pleasant type encountered
in *Persuasion* and the rougher, cruder kind (like Fanny Price's
father in *Mansfield Park*) is used to good effect in the novels.

A bare statement of the main theme of the novels cannot possibly convey the rich variety of the lesser characters. All belong
to much the same social class. There are no servants of either sex,
except as minor figures, no village gossips and worthies of the

earthy type and no vulgarians such as Fanny Burney used vigorously to portray. The amazing thing is that within such narrow limits there is such a rich diversity of personalities. Old Mr Woodhouse, Miss Bates and Mr and Mrs Elton in *Emma*; Lady Catherine de Bourgh and Mr Collins in *Pride and Prejudice*; Mrs Norris, the Bertram girls and Mr Rushworth in *Mansfield Park,* are a mere handful among many; the clergymen, too, are worth special attention, ranging from the serious to the fatuous.

When they first appeared the novels had their admirers and their detractors, and that has been the case ever since. The critics complained that they were commonplace and dull, while the enthusiasts praised their wit and charm. One reviewer remarked : 'It is no fool that can describe fools so well.'

Miss Mitford told Mr Austen-Leigh, the writer of the *Memoir* of his aunt, 'I would almost cut off one of my hands if it would enable me to write like your aunt with the other.'

In Lockhart's *Life of Scott* it is recorded that Sir Walter wrote in his diary for 14 March 1826, 'Read again for the third time at least Miss Austen's finely-written novel of *Pride and Prejudice.* That young lady has a talent for describing the involvements and feelings and characters of ordinary life which is to me the most wonderful I ever met with. The big Bow-Wow strain I can do myself like any going now; but the exquisite touch which renders ordinary, commonplace things and characters interesting from the truth of the description and the sentiment is denied to me. What a pity such a gifted creature died so early !'

Macaulay, the poet, essayist and critic, wrote : 'She has given us a multitude of characters, all, in a certain sense, commonplace, all such as we meet every day, yet they are all as perfectly discriminated from each other as if they were the most eccentric of human beings.'

On the other hand, Mrs Browning, the poet, thought her superficial, and that her characters had no soul.

Charlotte Brontë, as might be expected, also found her superficial : 'The passions are perfectly unknown to her; she rejects even a speaking acquaintance with that stormy sisterhood. What sees keenly, speaks aptly, moves flexibly, it suits her to study; but what throbs fast and full, though hidden, what the blood rushes through, what is the unseen seat of life, and the sentient target of death, this Miss Austen ignores.'

A justifiable comment! Those who are absorbed by the passions will probably avoid Miss Austen, who knew her own limitations well enough. But her admirers, among them many men, fully appreciate the verses written earlier this century by Rudyard Kipling, himself a master of story construction and character delineation :

Jane's Marriage

Jane went to Paradise;
    That was only fair.
Good Sir Walter[1] followed her,
    And armed her up the stair.
Henry[2] and Tobias[3],
    And Miguel[4] of Spain,
Stood with Shakespeare at the top
    To welcome Jane—

Then the Three Archangels
    Offered out of hand
Anything in Heaven's gift
    That she might command.
Azrael's eyes upon her,
    Raphael's wings above,
Michael's sword against her heart,
    Jane said : "Love".

Instantly the under-
    standing Seraphim
Laid their fingers on their lips
    And went to look for him.
Stole across the Zodiac,
    Harnessed Charles's Wain,
And whispered round the Nebulae
    "Who loved Jane?"

In a private limbo
    Where none had thought to look,
Sat a Hampshire gentleman
    Reading of a book.
It was called *Persuasion,*
    And it told the plain
Story of the love between
    Him and Jane

He heard the question
    Circle Heaven through—
Closed the book and answered :
    "I did—and do !"
Quietly but speedily

(as Captain Wentworth moved)
Entered into Paradise
The man Jane loved!

Jane lies in Winchester, blessed be her shade!
Praise the Lord for making her, and her for all she made.
And, while the stones of Winchester—or Milsom Street—remain,
Glory, Love, and Honour unto England's Jane!

[1] Sir Walter Scott—fellow novelist and great admirer of her work.

[2-3] Henry Fielding and Tobias Smollet—two great novelists of the earlier part of the eighteenth century.

[4] Miguel Cervantes—seventeenth century novelist and dramatist, creator of *Don Quixote*.

SEVEN
Elizabeth Barrett Browning

ELIZABETH MOULTON BARRETT (later Mrs Browning) was the earliest great woman poet. She was remarkable both in character and in her eventful life. She was the eldest child of a family of eleven— eight boys and three girls. Many people today know a little about her father and family, because her romantic marriage to Robert Browning has been used as the subject of at least one play. There has even been a successful musical about them, though the real Elizabeth and Robert appear to have had little interest in music, except in the words.

Elizabeth was born in 1806. She began to write verse before she was eight and continued to write until her death in 1861. She was, from an even earlier age, an avid reader, devouring books of any and every kind. Nor was her reading confined to English. She was fascinated by languages and when quite a young woman had learned Greek, Latin, Hebrew, French and Italian. It was fortunate that she enjoyed studying language and literature, for it was to be her great solace through the weary years of illness that were to follow.

Her early life was happily spent at their home, Hope End, near Malvern. In the beautiful countryside she stored up many precious memories that helped her when she became, as she said, 'a bird in a cage'. In Malvern lived Hugh Stuart Boyd, the blind scholar who encouraged Elizabeth's love and knowledge of Greek, which was already considerable, as she had shared her brothers' Greek lessons. At Hope End she had her first serious illness and an accident with her pony which left her with a severely strained and permanently weakened back. There, too, her mother died in 1828 and some time later the family went to live at Sidmouth for a few years.

It was, however, when Mr Barrett decided to live in London that the second stage of Elizabeth's development began. They knew no one when they arrived and Mr Barrett apparently was satisfied that it should be so. Fortunately a cousin of his, John Kenyon, introduced himself into the family and was keen that they, particularly Elizabeth, should meet his many literary friends. Mr Barrett disdained the offer and Elizabeth was merely terrified. She was shy and abnormally sensitive and the very thought of meeting strangers made her ill.

But at last the kind-hearted, middle-aged widower Kenyon persuaded her to meet Miss Mitford, as being an already well-known literary figure of her own sex.

Mary Russell Mitford was then in her fiftieth year and Elizabeth twenty years younger. They liked each other at once, although they realised their characters and tastes were very different. Miss Mitford was charmed by the 'delightful young creature who is so sweet and gentle and so pretty that one looks at her as if she were some bright flower'. Their friendship lasted until Miss Mitford's death. It was kept up chiefly by correspondence—sometimes several letters a week—because Miss Mitford could not often leave her country home owing to the claims of her father, to whose interests she was utterly devoted. Dr Mitford, although amiable, had extremely extravagant tastes and his daughter had to work harder and harder at her writing to help pay for his self-indulgence. But her love and admiration for him never seemed to falter. Elizabeth Barrett was just as devoted to her own father who, particularly after her mother's death, had a special—if wayward—affection for his eldest child.

Edward Moulton Barrett, descendant of a wealthy Jamaican family of slave-owners, looked on his children as his personal possessions—part of the furniture. So long as they obeyed his every whim, he loved them. He did not have much imagination, and when they settled in London he assumed that Elizabeth, then thirty years old, would stay passively in his care for the rest of her life. He was proud of her verses and had actually had some of them printed privately. But for him poetry was merely a way of passing the time.

To Elizabeth poetry was increasingly becoming life itself, an inner world of thought and feeling more real than the world outside. As her health grew worse and she had to lie in one room for many hours each day, she exercised her mind and spirit in reading, writing and meditation. Her illness made Mr Barrett feel even surer that she would always be happily dependent upon him and a willing subject to his rule, which was far less severe than that he imposed on his sons and younger daughters.

Hoping that a winter at the seaside would suit her better than London, Mr Barrett in 1839 sent Elizabeth and her brother Edward to Torquay. There tragedy overwhelmed her. Edward, the only brother who loved her with understanding, was accidentally drowned. Her grief over this loss was never fully healed. She was too ill to leave Torquay for many months and her low state is revealed in a letter to Miss Mitford :

'Can anything grow anywhere or any way with this terrible wind? The temperature of my bedroom is kept up day and night to 65° and I am not suffered to be moved from the bed even for its making—and yet the noxious character of the air makes me very uncomfortable and sleepless. I took two draughts of opium last night—but even the second failed to bring sleep. It *is* a blessed thing—that sleep—one of my worst sufferings being the want of it. Opium, opium, night after night—and some nights, during east winds, even opium won't do, you see !'

When she was able to return to London, she settled into a way of life which was bearable only because she read, poetry, novels, reviews, in fact anything that could be got. Sometimes, to ease sleeplessness, reading lasted throughout the night as well as the day. And, whenever she could hold her pen, she wrote—letters to friends, articles for the quarterly reviews and, of course, poetry. In pain herself, she was always worried about Miss Mitford, who was plagued by rheumatism. This is a typical letter :

'Dearest Miss Mitford, when you are out of your garden, do you sit a great deal? Now, at night—during those long watching, writing nights—against which there is no use remonstrating—do you sit them all? If you do—indeed, indeed, it is very bad for you. And it would be so wise if you would learn to be a *lollard* like me, and establish yourself on a sofa, instead of on a chair, and study the art, not a very difficult one, of writing in a recumbent position. I can write as well or as badly, when I lie down, as at a desk.'

This was advice from one who knew pain by experience.

She left an all-too-clear picture of conditions in her comfortable Victorian home. It is dated May 1843 : '... I have come into Papa's room, the adjoining one to mine, for the first time today—to have the windows opened and a little dusting done ... which

will make me cleaner and more exemplary tomorrow. The conse-
quence of living through the winter in one room, with a fire day
and night, and every crevice sealed close ... you may imagine perhaps ... At last we come to walk upon a substance like white sand
and if we don't lift our feet gently up and put them gently down
we ... stir up the sand into a cloud. As to a duster or a broom,
seen in profile even, calculate their effect upon us! The spiders
have grown tame and their webs are a part of our domestic
economy. The result of which is that I am glad May is come.'

The 'we' of whom she writes are her two closest companions, her
devoted personal maid, Wilson, and her spaniel Flush, a gift from
Miss Mitford. Flush loved Elizabeth freely, without any tinge of
pity or sense of duty, two things she quickly and sadly sensed in
her dealings with most human beings. Fittingly, her first verses were
lines in appreciation of Flush, with the characteristic footnote :
'This dog was the gift of my dear and admired friend, Miss Mitford, and belongs to the beautiful race she has rendered celebrated
among English and American readers. The Flushes have their
laurels as well as the Caesars—the chief difference (at least the very
head and front of it) consisting, perhaps, in the bald head of the
latter under the crown.'

The poem opens with a loving description of Flush's beauty, and
continues :

> Yet, my pretty, sportive friend,
> Little is't to such an end
>   That I praise thy rareness;
> Other dogs may be thy peers
> Haply in these drooping ears
>   And this glossy fairness.
>
> But of *thee* it shall be said,
> This dog watched beside a bed
>   Day and night, unweary,
> Watched within a curtained room
> Where no sunbeam brake the gloom
>   Round the sick and dreary.
>
> Roses, gathered for a vase,
> In that chamber died apace,
>   Beam and breeze resigning;
> This dog only, waited on,
> Knowing that when light is gone
>   Love remains for shining !

This dog, if a friendly voice
Call him now to blither choice
   Than such a chamber-keeping;
'Come out', praying from the door—
Presseth backwards as before,
    Up against me leaping.

Blessings on thee, dog of mine,
Pretty collars make thee fine,
   Sugared milk make fat thee!
Pleasures wag on in thy tail,
Hands of gentle motion fail
   Nevermore, to pat thee.

Whiskered cats anointed flee,
Sturdy stoppers keep from thee
   Cologne distillations;
Nuts be in thy path for stones,
And thy feast-day macaroons
   Turn to daily rations.

Mock I thee, in wishing weal?
Tears are in my eyes to feel
   Thou art made so straitly,
Blessing needs must straiten too—
Little can'st thou joy or do,
   Thou who lovest *greatly*.

Yet be blessed to the height
Of all good and all delight
   Pervious to thy nature;
Only *loved* beyond that line,
With a love that answers thine,
   Loving fellow-creature.

Two of her earliest published poems were written in dramatic form. One, *A Drama of Exile,* has something of Milton's spirit of reverence and grandeur. Outside Eden, in a desert place, Adam and Eve, watched over by Gabriel, are tempted by Lucifer. In their perplexity they see a vision of Christ and hear His promise of aid. The vision ends and they renew their vows of love to each other and are encouraged by a chorus of angels as they go further into the wilderness:

   Exiled human creatures,
     Let your hope grow larger!
   Larger grows the vision

Of the new delight.
From this chain of Nature's
    God is the Discharger,
And the Actual's prison
    Opens to your sight.

God, above the starlight,
    God above the patience,
Shall at last present ye
    Guerdons worth the cost.
Patiently enduring,
Painfully surrounded,
Listen how we love you,
    Hope the uttermost!
Waiting for that curing
    Which exalts the wounded,
Hear us sing above you—
    EXILED BUT NOT LOST!

The other, *The Seraphim*, was written and published earlier. It tells the drama of Christ's crucifixion in the words of two mighty seraphim, Ador the Strong and Zerah the Bright One, as they watch the scene from outside the Gates of Heaven.

These two poems made a very great impression in literary circles and were included in the first collected edition of her work published in 1844 and dedicated to her father.

In the Preface she wrote: '... while my poems are full of faults —as I go forward to my critics and confess—they have my heart and life in them, they are not empty shells. If it must be said of me that I have contributed immemorable verses to the many rejected by the age, it cannot at least be said that I have done so in a light and irresponsible spirit. Poetry has been as serious a thing to me as life itself; and life has been a very serious thing; there has been no playing at skittles for me in either ... I have done my work, not as mere hand and head work, apart from the personal being, but as the completest expression of that being to which I could attain.'

Her knowledge and appreciation of the earlier English poets is reflected in a long review she wrote of an anthology, *The Book of the Poets* for the *Athenaeum*. A unique contribution, also to the *Athenaeum*, was her account of the Greek Christian poets with her own sensitive translations in verse. A specialised form of the Greek language was used by these poets and this Miss Barrett had studied with particular interest.

By the time the 1844 poems were published, Elizabeth was in touch with many great men of letters of the day, although chiefly by correspondence. She had met the ageing William Wordsworth and the newly-risen star, Alfred Lord Tennyson. Thomas Carlyle and his wife Jane admired her, and Leigh Hunt and Walter Savage Landor wrote appreciatively of her work. John Kenyon, her cousin, who had used his own assured position to strengthen hers, was delighted that the invalid's interests were linked to the literary world where she so rightly belonged.

Yet the fact remained that she really knew very few people. Her ill-health and her father's dislike of callers at his house cut her off from the ordinary exchanges of life. She only knew men and women by what they *wrote,* and although this was often interesting and enjoyable, as her letters to Miss Mitford and others show, it was hardly satisfactory.

However, in 1845, she received her first letter of appreciation from Robert Browning, the young poet whose own work she greatly admired. She and Miss Mitford had already argued about him— Miss Mitford disliked his poems and everything she had heard of the poet himself. Encouraged by John Kenyon, Browning, after a number of letters had been exchanged, actually managed to get an invitation to visit Elizabeth. Already there was a bond of sympathy between them and their meeting only made it stronger. After that, to Miss Barrett's delight and consternation, Mr Robert Browning and his flowers came to her room twice a week. These visits were, fortunately, completely disregarded by Mr Barrett, to the half-terrified envy of her two sisters, Henrietta and Arabel.

How different was Robert Browning's understanding companionship from the attitude of some of the men who later thought ill of her! Such was opinion then that they felt that a woman should not be brought before the public by her writing. Indignantly she wrote to Miss Mitford of one such critic :

'Ever since my last book has brought me a little more before the public, I can do or say nothing right with him—and on and on he talks epigrams about the sin and shame of those divine angels called women, daring to tread in the dust of a multitude when they ought to be minding their clouds. All this, not a bit in joke, but gravely and bitterly . . . For a woman to hang down her head like a lily through life and "die of a rose in aromatic pain" at her death . . . and be "defended" by the strong and mighty thinkers on all sides of her—this, he thinks, is her destiny and glory.'

Frail in body, romantic in imagination and mystical in thought, all her Victorian life she believed strongly in every woman's right to think and act for herself. She did not believe men should dominate everything. Here, at least, she fully agreed with the sturdy Miss Mitford, who, however, went much further than Elizabeth was prepared to go. She once announced that 'marriages are the most foolish things under the sun', and it was fortunate for her father that this *was* her belief. But Elizabeth was having to consider marriage for herself.

Robert Browning soon made it clear that nothing would satisfy him but marriage with Elizabeth Barrett. She went through agonies of doubt and fear, unable to imagine that anyone, least of all this wonderful young genius, could think with anything but pity of so poor a creature as herself. Worn out with constant pain she was almost completely dependent on the services of others. But the family doctor became another ally, giving his firm opinion that her greatest need was not seclusion, but warmth and sunshine. He recommended her to spend the winter of 1845 in Italy. She was overjoyed at the prospect and, encouraged by Browning, began to go out for short drives whenever the weather was fine.

But there was 'a dead silence of Papa' to be reckoned with. Arrangements were made for travelling and all was prepared. Then the blow fell. She was forbidden to go. Despite her independent spirit, Elizabeth hated to displease the father she loved, and although bitterly disappointed she reluctantly agreed to try one more winter in England.

Browning, however, made her promise that if she came well through the winter she would marry him in the summer of 1846. Luckily, the winter was not severe; but Elizabeth's poems written then show her own sense of unfitness for such a marriage. In *Proof and Disproof* she wrote:

> I have known some bitter things—
>   Anguish, anger, solitude,
> Year by year an evil brings,
>   Year by year denies a good;
> March winds violate my springs,
> I have known how sickness bends,
>   I have known how sorrow breaks,
> How quick hopes have sudden ends,
>   How the heart thinks till it aches
> Of the smile of buried friends.
>
> Last, I have known *thee,* my brave
>   Noble thinker, lover, doer!

The best knowledge last I have.
But thou comest as the thrower
Of fresh flowers upon a grave.

Count what feelings used to move me;
Can this love assort with those?
Thou, who art so far above me,
Wilt thou stoop so for repose?
Is it true that thou canst love me?

No one in her family believed she would ever do anything but lie in her gloomy room and write poetry. She was, to them, a fixture in familiar surroundings, which nothing would change. They did not realise how often she had been able to smooth their own paths. Once she had arranged, in their father's absence, that they should all go to visit Miss Mitford in the country.

Later she wrote to Miss Mitford: 'Did you understand that the escapade yesterday was unknown to the High Priest here?—to Papa, I mean? Very wrong—yes, that is true. *You must not mention it!* A little overstrictness sometimes *drives* into temptation.'

Later, again: 'Yes—there is an excess of strictness. Too much is found objectionable and the result is that everything that *can* be done in an aside, *is* done, without too much consideration, perhaps, of the right and the wrong. Not that there is the least inclination to an over-wildness—I see nothing of such a thing—nothing. But— dear Papa's wishes would be consulted more tenderly if his commands were less straight and absolute. We are all dealt with alike, you know—and I do not pretend to more virtue than my peers.'

This point of view was the one she took about the crisis in her own life. She knew in her heart that if her father was told of her plans to marry, he would take the most extreme action a Victorian father could to stop it. Her brothers were not, on the whole, sympathetic to her, and her sisters, though loving, could not help.

In the end, she decided to tell no one until the marriage was over. She feared that if any of her friends knew beforehand, even Mr Kenyon, they might be accused of helping her. So one fine day in 1846, accompanied only by the faithful Wilson—and Flush—she married Robert Browning at Marylebone Church.

From then onward her life was transformed. The great shadows lifted. They went at once to Italy, travelling through Europe by easy stages. She was overjoyed—travel a new and wonderful pleasure. Sights and sounds, people and places quite familiar to other people, were all discoveries to her, and she revelled in them.

Naturally, she was often tired physically, but her husband's devotion was not only romantic, he was a resourceful and capable man and wanted nothing but her happiness. It was a perfect partnership until the day of her death fifteen years later.

When their friends were told of the marriage, everyone was highly delighted, and understood the reason for secrecy. Although Elizabeth sent an affectionate letter to her father he never replied. He never forgave her or wrote to her, although she continued to write letters to him. Her sisters told her secretly of his rage at the time, his refusal to hear her name mentioned in the house and, later on, how he treated Henrietta in the same way when she became engaged. However, he seemed satisfied with the way he had handled his daughters, so Elizabeth could feel—sadly—that her departure had not lost him too much sleep.

To Miss Mitford she had written : 'Have faith in me that I have struggled to do the right and the generous and not the selfish thing—although when you read this letter, I shall have given to one of the most gifted and admirable of men, a wife unworthy of him. I shall be the wife of Robert Browning. Against *you*—in allowing you no confidence . . . I have not certainly sinned, I think . . . so do not look at me with those reproachful eyes.'

In contrast to the Barrett family, Robert Browning's own father and sister were delighted at the marriage. The sister, Sarianna, became one of their most regular correspondents. The couple liked Italy so much that they decided to live there—first in Pisa and then in Florence, where their house, Cass Guidi, drew many famous visitors.

Only gradually did Elizabeth become used to the idea that Robert's love and understanding was based on admiration—not pity. Her feeling for him found expression in a group of sonnets which she thrust into his coat pocket one morning after breakfast. They were intimate and exquisite love poems which were not intended for any eye but his. Some years later, however, Robert persuaded her that poems of such beauty ought to be available for others to read. Eventually she agreed to their publication under the title, *Sonnets from the Portuguese*, which suggested that they were translations. This is one of the most familiar :

> How do I love thee? Let me count the ways.
> I love thee to the depth and breadth and height
> My soul can reach, when feeling out of sight
> For the end of Being and ideal Grace.
> I love thee to the level of every day's

Most quiet need, by sun and candlelight.
I love thee freely, as men strive for Right;
I love thee purely, as they turn from Praise.
I love thee with the passion put to use
In my old griefs, and with my childhood's faith.
I love thee with a love I seemed to lose
With my lost saints—I love thee with the breath,
Smiles, tears, of all my life!—and, if God choose,
I shall but love thee better after death.

This series of Sonnets is probably the best-known and most appreciated part of her work for readers today.

Now secure in her own happiness, however, she once satirised the kind of love that lesser men could offer a woman. In *A Man's Requirements* she wrote :

> Love me, Sweet, with all thou art,
>   Feeling, thinking, seeing;
> Love me in the lightest part,
>   Love me in full being.

and in this way the verse continues to its sudden ending :

> Thus, if thou wilt prove me, Dear,
>   Woman's love no fable,
> *I* will love *thee*—half a year—
>   As a man is able.

Her husband's satisfaction in his marriage is most unpoetically expressed in a postscript to one of his wife's letters : 'We are as happy as two owls in a hole, two toads under a tree stump; or any other queer two poking creatures that we let live, after the fashion of their black hearts, only Ba is fat and rosy; yes, indeed.' ('Ba' was the pet name by which Elizabeth was known to her family and closest friends.) In 1849 their happiness was completed by the birth of a son.

Before this event, however, the Brownings visited various Italian cities and became thrilled by Italian art. Elizabeth revelled in the sunshine and warmth and quickly took the Italian people to her heart. In the 1840s there was unrest in Italy, as in many parts of Europe. Most Italians sought liberation from the domination of the Austrian Empire. In those days Italy was a group of Austrian provinces, but everywhere men were dreaming of freedom, and of making a country and nation of their own. Mrs Browning was in full sympathy with their hopes but was greatly shocked by the shootings and assassinations that bedevilled the lovely cities. There was, at first, no leadership and no sense of unity among the would-be liberators. As she said, 'we know nothing of what people will do when they aspire to liberty'.

Another feature of Italian life that disturbed her was the willingness of many to live on the glorious past, to feel that with a heritage from men like Virgil, Cicero, Catullus, Caesar, Boccaccio, Dante, Petrarch, Michaelangelo, Raphael, nothing more was required :

> ... she takes no heed
> How one clear word would draw an avalanche
> Of living sons around her, to succeed
> The vanished generations ...
>
> So henceforth she would seem
> No nation, but the poet's pensioner,
> With alms from every land of song and dream.
>
> We do not serve the dead—the past is past.
> God lives, and lifts His glorious mornings up
> Before the eyes of man awake at last,
> Who put away the meats they used to sup,
> And down upon the dust of earth outcast
> The dregs remaining of the ancient cup,
> Then turn to wakeful prayer and worthy act.

These lines from Part I of *Casa Guidi Windows* show what she hoped for Italy's future. The poem's title suggests the onlooker who saw the struggle at close quarters. It is a commentary on the events which led in the end to the liberation of Italy and its birth as a kingdom under Victor Emmanuel. She describes the enthusiasm of the first stages :

> ... How we gazed
> From Casa Guidi windows while, in trains
> Of orderly procession—banners raised,
> And intermittent bursts of martial strains
> Which died upon the shout, as if amazed
> By gladness beyond music—they passed on !

But no leader emerged at first. The possibilities were there :

> ... But the teacher, where?
> From all these crowded faces, all alive,
>
> ... may we in no wise dare
> To put a finger out and touch a man,
> And cry, 'This is the leader !' What, all these !

Broad heads, black eyes—yet not a soul that ran
From God down with a message?

Come, appear, be found,
If pope or peasant, come!

Part I of the poem ends in 1848 with death and destruction and
no leader. Part II, written some three years later, still laments the
failure of the Florentines and the triumph of the all-powerful
Austrian armies in Italy. Yet the poet believes that the longed-for
liberation will come.

Casa Guidi Windows is a difficult poem for anyone not familiar
with the history of those troubled years. It shows a different kind
of subject and treatment from Elizabeth's lyrical and romantic
work. She wrote, 'I have a book coming out in England called
Casa Guidi Windows, which will prevent everybody else (except
you) from speaking to me again.' The poem contains some strong
criticisms of England for taking no active interest in Italy's struggles.

She was an ardent democrat and, unlike most English people,
she approved the election of Louis Napoleon (nephew of Bonaparte)
as head of the French State, and later, Emperor, because he was
the choice of the people themselves. They might have chosen
wrongly—he was certainly a dictator—but the will of the people
was the main thing.

Elizabeth was a revolutionary herself in many ways, but it was
always from a *personal* angle and she was unlikely to ally herself
with any particular party. She had a high estimate of Napoleon
Bonaparte as a man of power, and when his body was returned to
Paris from his place of exile in St Helena she wrote *Crowned and
Buried.* The poem first tells of his conquests and the price—loss of
liberty—that the French paid so willingly. Then, when he lost all,
they realised their own loss as a nation and were bitter. But that
feeling died, and

France kept her old affection
As deeply as the sepulchre the corpse.

So there was returned to Paris

A little urn—a little dust inside,
Which once outbalanced the large earth, albeit
Today a four-years child might carry it,
Sleek-browed and smiling, 'Let the burden bide.'

Even as in life he had claimed many lands so at last he made
good his claim

To a French grave—another kingdom won
The last, of few spans—by Napoleon.

The poet justifies him thus :

And if they asked for rights, he made reply,
'Ye have my glory'—and so, drawing round them
His ample purple, glorified and bound them
In an embrace that seemed identity.
He ruled them like a tyrant—true, but none
Were ruled like slaves; each felt Napoleon.

I do not praise this man; the man was flawed
For Adam—much more, Christ!—his knees unbent,
His hand unclean, his aspiration bent
Within a sword-sweep—pshaw—
. . . but since he had
The genius to be loved, why, let him have
The justice to be honoured in his grave.

I think this nation's tears thus poured together
Better than shouts. I think this funeral
Grander than crowning, though a Pope bless all.
I think this grave stronger than thrones. But whether
The crowned Napoleon or the buried clay
Be worthier, I discern not; angels may.

In 1848, 'The Year of Revolutions', Mrs Browning was moved
to anger and pity by all she heard of the sufferings of the poor in
England, because of the shortage of food caused by the Corn Laws.
In *The Cry of the Human,* she wrote :

The curse of gold upon the land
    The lack of bread enforces;
The rail-cars snort from strand to strand,
    Like more of Death's White Horses.

The rich preach 'rights' and 'future days',
    And hear no angel scoffing,
The poor die mute, with starving gaze
    On corn-ships in the offing.
        Be pitiful, O God.

Even earlier than this she had strongly protested against the
terrible treatment of little children employed in factories and
mines in England. *The Cry of the Children,* coming from the pen
of so influential a poet as Mrs Browning, brought home to many
the sufferings of those who could not speak for themselves :

They look up with their pale and sunken faces
    And their looks are sad to see,
For the man's hoary anguish draws and presses
    Down the cheeks of infancy.

'Your old earth,' they say, 'is very dreary,
    Our young feet,' they say, 'are very weak;
Few paces have we taken, yet are weary—
    Our grave-rest is very far to seek.

For all day we drag our burden tiring
    Through the coal-dark underground,
Or, all day, we drive the wheels of iron
    In the factories round and round.'

Do you hear the children weeping and disproving,
    O, my brothers, what ye preach?
For God's possible is taught by His world's loving,
    And the children doubt of each.

Later in her life, she was aroused to the horrors of slavery in America. She had met in Italy the famous American author of *Uncle Tom's Cabin*, Mrs Harriet Beecher Stowe, and had been greatly disturbed by what she said. When asked for a poem against slavery to be sent to an American anti-slavery publication, she produced *The Runaway Slave at Pilgrims' Point*, which, she said, might well be felt 'too ferocious'. It is indeed a terrible indictment of slavery.

At Pilgrims' Point, where long ago the Pilgrim Fathers had stepped ashore to build a nation devoted to freedom, the poet places the central figure, a negress slave. The negress tells her own story, of the white owners who killed her lover, a fellow-slave, and took her for their pleasure. She bore a white child who, as it lay in her arms, glanced up with the 'master's' look. In horror she smothered the child with her shawl and cursed the white man. This shocking and tragic poem was published first in America.

In 1851, at the height of her fame, Mrs Browning went with her husband and son on a long tour through Italy, Switzerland, France and then back home to England. In Paris she fulfilled one of her earlier ambitions by meeting a French writer she had long admired—George Sand. This was the more remarkable since that strange, masculine woman usually refused all interviews. Years earlier Elizabeth Barrett had written two sonnets addressed to George Sand, *A Desire* and *A Recognition*. She there hailed her as

Thou large-brained woman and large-hearted man,
   Self-called George Sand! whose soul, amid the lions
Of thy tumultous senses, moans defiance
   And answers roar for roar, as spirits can.

and again

True genius, but true woman! dost deny
The woman's nature with a manly scorn,
And break away the gauds and armlets worn
By weaker woman in captivity?
... and while before
The world thou burnest in a poet-fire,
We see thy woman-heart burn evermore
Through the large flame.

They met on several occasions. Each time she noted the strength and moral capacity of this woman—a woman who seemed to inspire admiration rather than love, and who shone as the *man* in the company of the young men who sat smoking with her, listening eagerly to her advice. Mrs Browning went to visit her once, risking her death of cold—she was always susceptible to chills of every kind—but declared that the visit was worth the risk.

She had dreaded coming home to England. All her past unhappiness would be stirred up, particularly the death of her beloved brother. But when they reached London they were welcomed everywhere, except, of course, in her own home. Robert's friends, notably Carlyle and Tennyson, were eager to tell her how much they admired her work. She told Miss Mitford she was 'very nearly killed by the climate and the kindness'.

On later visits to London she met Charles Kingsley, John Ruskin and Florence Nightingale, amongst other celebrities. There seems no record of her meeting Dickens but she loved his books, even though he must always rank, with her, below Victor Hugo. She valued Tennyson's poetry so highly, that she and Robert were gratified and amused when the Laureate, as he then was, came to their London apartment armed with his latest poem, *Maud*. After a meal, fortified by port and tobacco, he read the whole poem aloud, pausing at frequent intervals to admire the beauty of a passage or the aptness of his own phrases. At last, he rose to go at 2.30 a.m.

Mrs Browning's passion for novels remained and one of her few complaints of life in Italy was that new boks took so long to arrive. She could hardly wait to open the pages of *Jane Eyre* which, as

ELIZABETH BARRETT BROWNING

soon as read, she declared must be the work of a woman. She wrote with great appreciation of Mrs Gaskell and, most of all, of George Eliot whom she met in Rome.

Her own last work was a poem of major importance—a novel in verse form. This had long been her ambition and in it she wished not only to tell a story, but to express a lifetime of thought and experience.

'A few characters—a simple story—and plenty of room for passion and thought—*that* is what I want . . . where is the obstacle to making as interesting a story of a poem as of a prose work— echo answers, *where*? Conversations and events, why may they not be given as rapidly and passionately and lucidly in verse as in prose—echo answers, *why*?' Earlier she had experimented with a poem-novel, *Lady Geraldine's Courtship,* which had been much admired by Carlyle and the public in general but had not satisfied herself. Modern readers often find it over-sentimental and unconvincing.

Aurora Leigh is a long and complex tale, told in the first person by Aurora, the heroine, who has much in common with the poet herself. She is determined not to lose her own personality, even for the sake of love. She must be accepted for what she is, rather than as the figure of a lover's imagination or wishes. Her lover and cousin, Romney Leigh, a man devoted to good works, long imagined that he had only to propose marriage and she would agree to share his life and work. But she replied,

> You misconceive the question, like a man,
> Who sees a woman as the complement
> Of his sex merely. You forget too much
> That every creature, female as the male,
> Stands single in responsible act and thought
> As also in birth and death. Whoever says
> To a loyal woman, 'Love and work with me',
> Will get fair answers if the work and love,
> Being good themselves, are good for her—the best
> She was born for . . . But *me* your work
> Is not the best for—nor your love the best,
> Nor able to commend the kind of work
> For love's sake merely.

By the time the story ends, both have experienced suffering and learned much. They were, after all, suited to each other, after their experiences of life. Mrs Browning, happily married herself, could find no better destiny for her heroine than a happy marriage.

105

Romney had at first planned to marry Marian, a young and innocent girl whom he could rescue from a life of misery and possible
shame. He felt moved by social justice, rather than love. But the
power of evil appears in the shape of the treacherous Lady Waldemar, who wanted Romney for herself. She made havoc of his plan
and the young girl's happiness by persuading Marian not to come
to church for the wedding since he did not truly love her. Too late
Aurora realised her treachery. She cries out, as if Romney were
present:

> She'll not be thwarted by an obstacle
> So trifling as her souls is . . . much less yours.
> Is God a consideration?—she loves you,
> Not God; she will not flinch for Him indeed;
> She loves you, sir, with passion, to lunacy;
> She loves you like her diamonds—almost.

She rails against those who are wrongly called 'good'

> . . . and we have all known
> Good critics who have stamped out poet's hope,
> Good statesmen who pulled ruin on the State,
> Good patriots who for a theory risked a cause,
> Good kings who disembowelled for a tax,
> Good popes who brought all good to jeopardy,
> Good Christians who sat still in easy chairs
> And damned the general world for standing up.
> Now may the good God pardon all good men.
> How bitterly I speak.

One of the best passages in the poem—which is rather full of
digressions and philosophical comments—is the description of the
scene in the church, as the congregation waits for the bride who
does not appear. On the one side are the rich, prosperous friends
of the bridegroom, and on the other the noisy crowd of people
from the poor streets where the bride had lived and the bridegroom had worked. The rich but vulgar-minded spectators mutter:

> They say the bride's a mere child, who can't read,
> But knows the things she shouldn't, with wide-awake
> Great eyes. I'd go through fire to look at her.
> . . . Yes, yes, this Leigh
> Was always odd; it's in the blood, I think,
> His father's Uncle's cousin second son
> Was, was . . . you understand me; and for him
> He's stark—has turned quite lunatic upon
> This modern question of the poor—the poor.

An excellent subject when you're moderate;
You've seen Prince Albert's model lodging-house?
Does honour to His Royal Highness. Good.
But would he stop his carriage in Cheapside
To shake a common fellow by the fist
Whose name was ... Shakespeare? No, we draw a line,
And if we stand not by our order, we
In England, we fall headlong. Here's a sight,
A hideous sight, a most indecent sight!
(pointing to the poor rabble crowding into the church)

To treat as equals, 'tis anarchical;
It means more than it says; 'tis damnable.
Why, sir, we can't have even our coffee good
Unless we strain it.

Because of the treachery of Lady Waldemar, the unhappy bride
went to France where she fell into evil hands. She had a child and
lived as an outcast until Aurora found her and listened with horror
to her tale. Believing that Lady Waldemar had tricked Romney
into marriage, she took Marian and her child to Italy. Romney
found them and declared that he had never imagined a marriage
with Lady Waldemar; he insisted that his wife must be Marian
and no one else. Marian, absorbed in her child, had guessed
Aurora's secret love for Romney, and so she refused his offer.
So, despite Aurora's success as a writer in London, she was grateful
for the love that Romney said had been hers since first they met.

The poem is an interesting experiment, full of memorable passages, satire, spiritual truth and worldly wisdom, but too often they
slow up or interrupt the continuity of the tale. It was published in
1856 and aroused immediate interest and controversy. Many people
were shocked by the story of Marian and the author's outspoken
sympathy for the victims of vice and corruption. They believed
that no 'good' woman should know of such things: to write of
them was to outrage decency. Mothers forbade their daughters to
read the poem, but many did. It is certain that they could come
to no harm from anything that Mrs Browning wrote, for she was
always a champion of truth and purity and the opponent of hypoc-
risy and cruelty.

When her old friend and cousin John Kenyon died, he left very
handsome sums of money to both Robert and Elizabeth whose first
meeting he had helped to bring about. So the Brownings not only
had great fame but also a much easier time in the last years of
Elizabeth's life, a time spent at Casa Guidi in great happiness.

They were visited by many friends, including William Makepeace Thackeray, and enjoyed each other's company until Elizabeth's death in 1861.

She was buried in Florence. On the walls of Casa Guidi her Florentine friends put a marble slab, on which they recorded their affection and gratitude for one who, by her verse, had united Italy and England within a golden ring.

EIGHT
Mary Russell Mitford

THIS KINDLY, stout-hearted lady has already been introduced as
someone who used to receive letters from Elizabeth Barrett Browning, her junior by twenty years. But she was very much more than
that, as her story shows.

She was born in the reign of George III, in 1787, the daughter
of parents of good family and difficult natures. Her mother was
wealthy and indolent. Her father was a qualified doctor, who
seldom practised, and a born gambler and spendthrift. As a small
child Mary was happy and lively and soon displayed a great appe-
tite for reading and stories of every kind. Gradually her mother's
fortune was gambled away, and her father went off to London to
see if his luck would turn there. It did not, and his wife and
daughter joined him when they no longer had enough money from
him to stay at home.

On her tenth birthday, Mary went walking in London with her
father who bought her a public lottery ticket as a birthday present.
Their luck turned—she won no less than £20,000! At once all
their debts were paid, they bought a large house at Reading and
sent Mary to one of the few good boarding schools for girls. There
she studied the classics and modern literature, developed a particular taste for drama and became familiar with the work of the
great dramatists, ancient and modern.

Meantime, Dr Mitford had bought a large estate near Reading
and was enjoying the life of a country squire and county magistrate. But his hobbies were expensive—coursing in the country and
gambling in London. All this gradually reduced Mary's £20,000 to

nothing. Once again they were ruined. The big estate was sold up, and the family, by Dr Mitford's own choice, moved to a little labourer's cottage in the village of Three Mile Cross, a short distance from their old, luxurious home. Mrs Mitford was ill and growing feebler. Nothing was to be hoped from Dr Mitford, so Mary decided that she must try to earn money by writing. With great courage and determination she soon made headway but it was hard work and there was no one at first to encourage her or use any influence on her behalf.

At the same time she had to make friends with the village people. At first, the villagers resented 'the magistrate' and his house-hold who had descended uninvited in their midst. But Mary Mitford, rosy-faced and cheerful, brisk in manner, direct and friendly in approach, soon became beloved by everyone and 'belonged' to the village in a special sense. And the village proved to be her greatest benefactor.

She tried various kinds of writing, articles on general literary subjects and dramas which, though well-written, and produced by several leading actors of the day, were too gloomy to be popular. But, while doing this, she found a new subject—the village itself.

She sent several sketches of country life to *The Lady's Magazine* at the end of the year in 1822 and they were an immediate success. The circulation of the magazine rose from 250 to 2,000 copies a month. Jaded town-dwellers, living in the grime and smoke of industry, were refreshed by Mary Mitford's lively accounts of the fields, lanes and cottages, the animals and the people amongst whom she lived. The secret of her charm was an open one for all to know :

'I always wrote on the spot, and at the moment, and in nearly every instance with the closest and most resolute fidelity to the place and people; painting their failures and the many virtues of the villagers, under an intense and thankful conviction that, in every condition of life, goodness and happiness may be found by those who seek them, and never more surely than in the fresh air, the shade and the sunshine of nature.'

Such a belief was perfectly natural to one who thought it a privilege and never a burden to work for years to support an incurably extravagant parent, and to pay his debts after his death. The country articles, however, were her delight and fortunately they brought her not only admirers from all walks of life but also pounds, shillings and pence. For ten years she regularly chronicled the affairs of *Our Village* until she decided she could no longer find fresh material. However, because the public demand for her tales was so great, she had to extend her range to include accounts of other villages and some of her aristocratic friends in the great houses nearby. In this way Mary Mitford became the first of a long and still flourishing line of contributors who enliven newspapers and journals with 'nature' and country articles.

These sketches were only a part of her regular literary output but they were to prove the most lasting. A collection of some of the most popular articles was edited to form the book *Our Village* so that their permanency was ensured. Several editions have since been published and the book has become the classic that many of her friends prophesied. Other writers, particularly women, have used a village as the setting for very charming tales—but Mary Russell Mitford was the pioneer.

It is pleasant to think how warmly she was welcomed by her literary friends on her rare visits to London. In the country too, her cottage home and garden was the mecca for scores of people of every class who admired her writing and enjoyed her friendship.

She was helped by some of her wealthy friends to pay off her father's debts and she also received a royal bounty in acknowledgement of her work. For many years of her life she suffered badly from rheumatism which crippled her increasingly and she had several falls which made matters worse. But her cheerful spirit never failed and in her dying days she was tenderly cared for by her friends and neighbours.

The following extracts from *Our Village* are the best introduction to anyone who does not already know it. The opening paragraphs charmingly sum up her 'philosophy' : 'Of all situations for a constant residence, that which appears most delightful to me is a little village far in the country; a small neighbourhood, not of fine mansions finely peopled, but of cottages and cottage-like houses . . . with inhabitants whose faces are as familiar to us as the flowers in our garden; a little world of our own, close-packed and insulated like ants in an ant-hill, or bees in a hive, or sheep in a fold, or nuns in a convent, or sailors in a ship; where we know everyone, are known to everyone, interested in everyone, and authorised to hope that everyone feels an interest in us . . .

'Even in books I like a confined locality, and so do the critics when they talk of the unities. Nothing is so tiresome as to be whirled half over Europe at the chariot wheels of a hero, to go to sleep in Vienna and awaken at Madrid; it produces a real fatigue, a weariness of spirit. On the other hand, nothing is so delightful as to sit down in a country village in one of Miss Austen's delicious novels, quite sure before we leave it to become intimate with every spot and every person it contains.'

This point of view was quite the opposite to that held by Mrs Browning. She enjoyed foreign travel and, while admitting that Jane Austen's novels were good so far as they went, did not enjoy them because the characters all seemed to her completely without soul. Miss Mitford had something of Jane Austen's shrewd appreciation of the oddities of human nature, but she tended to view everyone, from her father down to the most mischievous village lad through rose-coloured spectacles.

She loved her garden : 'The pride of my heart and the delight of my eyes is my garden. Our house, which is in dimensions very like a bird-cage, and might, with almost equal convenience, be laid on a shelf or hung up in a tree, would be utterly unbearable in warm weather, were it not that we have a retreat out of doors— and a very pleasant retreat it is . . . Fancy a small plot of ground, with a pretty low irregular cottage at one end; a large granary divided from the dwelling by a little court running along one side; and a long, thatched shed, open towards the garden, and supported by wooden pillars, on the other. The bottom is bounded, half by an old wall and half by an old paling, over which we see a pretty distance of woody hills.

'The house, granary, wall and paling are covered with vines, cherry-trees, roses, honeysuckles and jessamines, with great clusters of tall hollyhocks running up between them; a large elder over-hanging the little gate, and a magnificent bay-tree, such a tree as shall scarcely be matched in these parts, breaking with its beautiful conical form the horizontal lines of the buildings. This is my garden; and the long pillared shed, the sort of rustic arcade, which runs along one side, parted from the flower-beds by a row of rich geraniums, is our out-of-door drawing room.'

Elsewhere she describes her geraniums : 'the very pear-tree [is] half-concealed by a splendid pyramid of geraniums, erected under its shade. Such geraniums! It does not become us poor mortals to be vain—but really, my geraniums! There is certainly nothing but the garden into which Aladdin found his way, and where the fruit was composed of gems, that can compare with them.'

One, at least, of these splendid plants was sent to Elizabeth Barrett, early in their acquaintance; according to her letter of thanks, it was a very welcome gift to the invalid in her shrouded, dusty room. Whatever Mary Mitford may once have said to

Elizabeth Barrett against marriage, she always had the liveliest interest in the young couples of the village. Her sympathy could be relied on if anything seemed to be going wrong with their love affairs. She gives a brief and delightful glimpse of one pair, Jem and Mabel hoeing in Farmer Thorpe's wheat field : 'Jem, with his bright complexion, his curling hair, his clear blue eyes and his trim figure—set off to great advantage by his short jacket and trousers and new straw hat; Mabel, with her little stuff gown, and her white handkerchief and apron—and her black eyes flashing from under a deep bonnet lined with pink . . . Their mutual admiration is clear enough in their work; but it speaks still more plainly in their idleness. Not a stroke have they done for these five minutes; Jem, propped on his hoe and leaning across the furrow, whispering soft nonsense; Mabel, blushing and smiling—now making believe to turn away—now listening, and looking up with a sweeter smile than ever, and a blush that makes her bonnet-lining pale . . .

'Now they are going to work again—no!—after three or four strokes the hoes have somehow become entangled and without either advancing a step nearer the other, they are playing with these rustic implements as pretty a game of romps—showing off as nice a piece of rural flirtation—as ever was exhibited since wheat was hoed.'

But Farmer Thorpe has arrived and 'Jem and Mabel have been parted; they are now at opposite sides of the field—he looking very angry, working rapidly and violently, and doing more harm than good—she looking tolerably sulky and just moving her hoe, but evidently doing nothing at all. Farmer Thorpe, on his part, is standing in the middle of the field, observing, but pretending not to observe, the little humours of the separated lovers. There is a lurking smile above the corners of his mouth that bespeaks him more amused than angry. He is a kind person after all and will certainly make no mischief.'

She also liked the village boys, particularly the mischievous ones. 'I plead guilty to a strong partiality towards that unpopular class of being, country boys. I have a large acquaintance amongst them, and I can almost say that I know good of many and harm of none. In general they are an open, spirited, good-humoured race, with a proneness to embrace the pleasures and eschew the evils of their condition, a capacity for happiness, quite unmatched in man or woman or girl.

'They are patient, too, and bear their fate as scapegoats (for all sins whatsoever are laid, as matters of course, to their door) whether at home or abroad, with amazing resignation; and considering the many lies of which they are the objects, they tell wonderfully few in return. The worst that can be said of them is that they seldom, when grown to man's estate, keep the promise of their boyhood; but that is a fault to come—a fault that may not come and ought not to be anticipated.'

She found them most interesting of all when playing cricket, unaware of her scrutiny.

That universal talking-point, the weather, is constantly used by the writer, with a country-dweller's awareness of its importance to those who work on the land. This picture of a wet summer introduces *The Haymakers*:

'Last summer was, as most of my readers probably remember, one of no small trial to haymakers in general, the weather being what is politely and gently termed "unsettled", which, in this pretty climate of ours, during "the leafy month of June", may commonly be construed into cloudy, stormy, drizzly, cold. In this instance the silky, courtly, flattering epithet, being translated, could hardly mean other than wet—fixed, determined, settled rain. From morning to night the clouds were dripping; roses stood tottering on their stalks; strawberries lay sopping in their beds; cherries and currants hung all forlorn on their boughs, with the red juice washed out of them; gravel roads turned into sand; pools into ponds; ditches into rivulets; rivers overflowed their channels; and that great evil, a summer flood, appeared inevitable. "The rain it raineth every day" was the motto for the month. Sheridan's wicked interpolation in Mr Coleridge's tragedy, "drip, drip, drip, there's nothing here but dripping", seemed made expressly for the season. Cut or uncut, the grass was spoiling; the more the hay was made, the clearer it appeared that it would never make to any purpose; the poor cattle shook their ears as if aware of an impending scarcity; salt, the grand remedy for sopped hay, rose in the market; farmers fretted; and gentlemen fumed.'

From this it seems clear that even in the good old days 'flaming June' could be a misnomer.

By way of contrast an extract from *The Hard Summer* must surely make the modern reader thankful that even very minor roads today are surfaced so as to be free from dust: 'What a dusty world it was, when about sunset we became cool enough to creep into it! Flowers in the court looking fit for a *hortus siccus*; mummies of plants, dried as in an oven; hollyhocks, once pink, turned into Quakers; cloves smelling of dust. Oh dusty world!

May herself looked of that complexion; so did Lizzie; so did all the houses, windows, chickens, children, trees and pigs in the village; so above all did the shoes. No foot could make three plunges into that abyss of pulverised gravel, which had the impudence to call itself a hard road, without being clothed with a coat a quarter of an inch thick. Woe to white gowns! Woe to black! Drab was your only wear.

'Then, when we were out of the streets, what a toil it was to mount the hill, climbing with weary steps and slow upon the brown turf by the wayside, slippery, hot, and hard as a rock! And then if we happened to meet a carriage coming along the middle of the road—the bottomless middle—what a sandy whirlwind it was! What choking! What suffocation! No state could be more pitiable, except indeed that of the travellers who carried this misery about with them.

'I shall never forget the plight in which we met the coach one evening in last August, full an hour after its time, steeds and driver, carriage and passengers, all one dust. The outsides, and the horses and the coachman seemed reduced to a torpid quietness, the resignation of despair. They had left off trying to better their condition and taken refuge in a wise and patient hopelessness, bent to endure in silence the extremity of ill. The six inside, on the contrary, were still fighting against their fate, vainly struggling to ameliorate their hapless destiny. They were visibly grumbling at the weather, scolding at the dust, and heating themselves like a furnace by striving against the heat. How well I remember the fat gentleman within his coat, who was wiping his forehead, heaving up his wig, and certainly uttering that ejaculation which, to our national reproach, is the phrase of our language best known on the continent.

'And that poor boy, red hot, all in a flame, whose mamma, having divested herself of all superfluous apparel, was trying to relieve his sufferings by the removal of his neckerchief—an operation which he resisted with all his might. How perfectly I remember him, as well as the pale girl who sat opposite, fanning herself with her bonnet into an absolute fever! They vanished after a while into their own dust; but I have them all before my eyes at this moment, a comparison picture to Hogarth's "Afternoon," a standing lesson to the grumblers at cold summers.'

The May (short for Mayflower) mentioned above was the name of Miss Mitford's white greyhound, the sole survivor of her father's kennels from more prosperous days and her constant companion.

Lizzie was the small daughter of the village carpenter who often went out with Miss Mitford on her walks. She was 'the plaything and queen of the village, a child three years old according to the register, but six in size and strength and intellect, in power and in self-will. She manages everybody in the place, the schoolmistress included; turns the wheeler's children out of their own little cart and makes them draw her; seduces cakes and lollipops from the very shop-window, makes the lazy carry her, the silent talk to her, the grave romp with her; does anything she pleases; is absolutely irresistible. Her chief attraction lies in her exceeding power of loving, and her firm reliance on the love and indulgence of others.'

May, the greyhound, had befriended a mongrel, Dash. Dash often used to come on these outings : 'Dash is a sort of a kind of a spaniel; at least there is in his mongrel composition some sign of that beautiful race. Besides his ugliness, which is of the worst sort—that is to say, the shabbiest—he has a limp on one leg that gives a peculiarly one-sided awkwardness to his gait; but independently of his great merit in being May's pet, he has other merits which serve to account for that phenomenon—being beyond all comparison, the most faithful, attached, and affectionate animal that I have ever known; and that is saying much. He seems to think it necessary to atone for his ugliness by extra good conduct, and does so dance on his lame leg, and so wag his scruffy tail, that it does anyone who has a taste for happiness good to look at him—so that he may now be said to stand on his own footing.'

Here now is a picture of Miss Mitford herself, on this occasion not only with May, but with no less a person than her father. It is late September and they are 'nutting'. Dr Mitford has hooked down with his walking-stick some of the tall hazel boughs clustered with nuts so that his daughter can reach them.

'I doffed my shawl, tucked up my flounces, turned my straw bonnet into a basket, and began gathering and scrambling—for, manage it how you may, nutting is scrambling work—those boughs, however tightly you may grasp them by the young fragrant twigs and the bright green leaves, will recoil and burst away . . . so on we go, scrambling and gathering with all our might and all our glee. Oh, what an enjoyment. All my life long I have had a passion for that sort of seeking which implies finding (the secret, I believe, of the love of field sports, which is in man's mind a natural impulse) —therefore I love violeting—therefore when we had a fine garden, I used to love to gather strawberries and cut asparagus, and, above all, to collect the filberts from the shrubberies; but this hedge-row nutting beats that sport all to nothing. That was a make-believe thing compared to this; there was no surprise, no suspense, no un-expectedness—it was as inferior to this wild nutting, as the turning out of a bag-fox is to unearthing the fellow, in the eyes of a staunch fox-hunter.'

Here we will leave Miss Mitford, full of the joy of life and as yet untroubled by the physical handicaps that plagued her later years.

NINE

Mrs Gaskell

ELIZABETH CLEGHORN STEVENSON was born in Chelsea in 1810, but brought up in Knutsford, Cheshire. Her mother died when she was very young and Elizabeth was sent to live with her much-loved aunt Lumb in Knutsford, the little country town she has immortalised as *Cranford*. She was well educated at a school in Stratford-upon-Avon and while still young showed the social qualities and graces that were to charm people throughout her life. She was pretty to watch and fun to talk to. She had a naturally serene and sympathetic nature and a gentle irony that was the salt of her comedy when she began to write.

Her relatives on both sides were cultured and well-to-do—like the characters in her domestic novels—and with them she was always a welcome visitor. She returned to London for two years before her marriage, spending most of the time nursing her father in his long last illness. Her step-mother had her own children and was not fond of Elizabeth, who gladly went back to Knutsford when her father died.

When she was twenty-one she married the Reverend William Gaskell, then assistant minister at a large Unitarian church in Manchester. Manchester lay barely twenty miles from Knutsford, but it was a totally different world. The churchgoers were mostly wealthy industrialists whose power and pride in the city were enormous. The noisy cotton-mills were in full production and their profits had set up a new aristocracy of wealth never dreamed of before. There was, indeed, an under-current of discontent among the poor, ill-paid workers, the 'hands' whose labours produced the wealth. Sometimes, machinery was wrecked. The Trade Union movement had already begun, but 'combination' was illegal, and progress very slow.

Young Mrs Gaskell was amazed at the contrasts she saw in the city. Unconsciously her memory—as it had always done—was storing up the strange, new kinds of people and ways of life she encountered. She was a good housewife and an untiring aid to her husband in their many church activities. As the years passed and her children were born—four daughters and one son—it seemed there could be room for nothing more in her busy life. Then, in 1844, sorrow came suddenly upon her; their little boy died and Elizabeth Gaskell was inconsolable.

At last, almost in despair, her husband suggested that she might find comfort in getting to know more about the wretched lives of the mill-workers. He, like many other enlightened men, felt that the whole country must be told of the shocking conditions in the mills. He knew, too, that his wife's sympathies were strong, because she herself knew some of the poor workers and their families. It proved to be the resource she needed. Out of her own sorrow and her sympathy with the downtrodden came *Mary Barton* (1848), one of the first novels to stand up for the industrial workers.

Mrs Gaskell's whole mind and heart were in her writing, she *must* represent the people as she knew them. She said of it afterwards: 'In *Mary Barton* nobody and nothing was real but the character of John Barton; the circumstances are different but the character and some of the speeches are exactly those of a poor man I know . . . I told the story according to a fancy of my own to really *see* the scenes I tried to describe (and they *were* as real as my own life at the time) and then to tell them, as nearly as I could, as if I were speaking to a friend over the fire on a winter's night.'

And again, when a friend challenged her to admit being the author (she had written under the name 'Cotton Mather Mills') she wrote: 'I did write it, but how did you find it out? I *do* want it to be concealed if possible, and I don't think anybody here has the least idea who is the author. I am almost frightened at my own action in writing it . . . I can only say I wanted to represent the subject in the light in which some of the workmen certainly consider it to be *true;* not that I dare to say it is the abstract, absolute truth.'

The story tells of John Barton, an embittered factory worker, who demanded a charter of liberties for workers. With his friends he marched to London to present the Charter to Parliament, who rejected it. His hatred of the employers leads to the final tragedy when he is driven to murder. The love story of his daughter, Mary, runs through the book, containing tragedy and happiness in the end, and above all, there is the loyalty and self-sacrifice which people will show even in the most wretched conditions.

The results of the publication of *Mary Barton* in 1848 were startling. Great indignation was aroused in Mr Gaskell's congregation and in many Manchester circles by a book which, they affirmed, was disgracefully unfair to the masters. Not all factory owners were cruel and crafty. Indeed they were not, although fair-minded ones were in the minority. But the public conscience was pricked, as it was to be again a little later by Dickens' *Hard Times* on a similar theme. Mrs Gaskell became very unhappy at the storm she had raised, but, on the other hand, she was praised and honoured by several notable writers. Thomas Carlyle for one wrote : 'Dear Madam (for I catch the *treble* of that fine, melodious voice very well),

'We have read your book here, my wife first and then I; both of us with real pleasure . . . your field is, moreover, new, important, full of rich material which (as is usual) required a soul of true opulence to recognise it as such . . .

'I gratefully accept it as a real contribution (about the first real one) towards developing a huge subject, which has lain dumb too long, and really ought to speak for itself and tell us its meaning a little, if there be any voice in it at all.'

Charles Dickens himself was quick to see the timelessness of the book, and the literary qualities of its author. He invited her to become a contributor to *Household Words,* of which he was editor. Meantime, the book was being widely read and the tears shed by its readers over the sufferings of the factory workers turned to protests against the conditions in which they worked.

Mary Barton is seldom read today. To us, it appears over-loaded with misery and unbalanced as a novel. But it achieved its purpose, and as a piece of graphic documentary evidence it has its place in social history.

It also made Mrs Gaskell a literary celebrity. She regularly contributed short stories to *Household Words,* and before long Dickens called her his 'Scheherezade', after the famous story-teller of *The Thousand and One Nights.* She enjoyed inventing stories, loved ghosts and mysteries and had a wide range of plots from comic to tragic. They came to her easily, and working on them made a pleasant change from domestic routine.

Short stories were well-paid too, but her husband took charge of all her earnings as a matter of course. She wrote to a friend that she had just received £10, 'and William has composedly buttoned it up in his pocket. He has promised I may have some for my Refuge'. Yet, some years later, when she was asked to sign a petition in support of the Married Women's Property Bill she was very doubtful and signed with considerable misgiving.

Mr Gaskell was a considerate Victorian husband. He rarely interfered with his wife's activities, and himself worked from dawn to dusk writing pamphlets and articles, both as a minister and public man in Manchester. Equally, Mrs Gaskell was no ardent feminist. She enjoyed an extremely active life, whether social, literary or domestic, and stayed firmly in charge of her home and her four daughters. She did her writing in the dining-room which had three doors opening into other parts of the house, so that she could easily keep in touch with what was going on around her.

Later, when writing the *Life of Charlotte Brontë,* she described how Charlotte was not only a famous novelist, but responsible for the running of the Parsonage and the comfort of its inhabitants. It was easier for a man to be an author : 'When a man becomes an author, it is probably merely a change of employment to him. He takes a portion of that time which has hitherto been devoted to some other study or pursuit; he gives up something of the legal or medical profession in which he has hitherto endeavoured to serve others, or relinquishes part of the trade or business by which he has been striving to gain a livelihood; and another merchant or lawyer or doctor steps into his vacant place, and probably does as well as he.

'But no other can take up the quiet, regular duties of the daughter, the wife or the mother, as well as she whom God hath appointed to fill that particular place; a woman's principal work in life is hardly left to her own choice; nor can she drop the domestic charges devolving on her as an individual for the exercise of the most splendid talents that were ever bestowed. And yet she must not shrink from the extra responsibility implied by the very fact of her possessing such talents.'

Mrs Gaskell enjoyed everything she did. Her visits to London put her in touch with many interesting people and she loved to talk to them about all kinds of subjects. She wrote : 'I wish I could help talking to men so much more than to women and I wish I could help men talking to me; but I believe we've a mutual attraction of which Satan is the originator.'

In the years after the publication of *Mary Barton* she had two serials in *Household Words, Cranford* from 1851 to 1853, when it was published in book form and *North and South* in 1853. *North and South* was another novel about Manchester, disguised as 'Milton' in the book. It is a much better balanced novel than *Mary Barton*, and thought by many critics to be her best. It shows the contrast and some of the conflict between two vastly different ways of life : between the industrial, smoky North of England, and the South with its older culture and its difficult agricultural conditions. Again, there is conflict between owners and workers in the mills, a problem that Mrs Gaskell had already faced.

In *North and South* it is seen through the eyes of Margaret Hale; Margaret was abruptly transferred by unhappy family circumstances from an idyllic life in a Hampshire village to the noise and crudity of Milton. The development of Margaret's character is shown against the stormy struggle between the early Trade Unionists and the reluctant mill owners.

In this book, however, a new type of owner is shown—a young man, self-opinionated and stubborn but ready to try to improve worker relations and conditions in his factory. His encounters with the dedicated workers' leader, and the conflicting ideas of moderate and violent elements among the workers, make for tension and drama as the hotheads seize control. But John Thornton, the owner, and Nicholas Higgins, the strike-leader, achieve a mutual respect and at least a partial understanding of each other's problems. Higgins had been badly misjudged by Thornton :

'Yo've called me impudent and a liar and a mischief-maker, and yo' might ha' said wi' some truth as I was now and then given to drink. And I ha' called you a tyrant, and an ould bull-dog, and a hard, cruel master; that's where it stands. But for th' childer, Measter, do yo' think we can e'er get on together?'

'Well!' said Mr Thornton, half-laughing, 'it was not my proposal that we should go together. But there's one comfort, on your own showing. We neither of us can think much worse of the other than we do now.'

'That's true,' said Higgins, reflectively. 'I've been thinking ever sin' I saw you what a mercy it was yo' didna tak me on, for I ne'er saw a man whom I could less abide. But that's, maybe, a hasty judgment; and work's work, to such as me. So, Measter, I'll come; and what's more, I thank yo', and that's a deal from me,' said he, more frankly, suddenly turning round and facing Mr Thornton fully for the first time.

'And that's a deal from me,' said Mr Thornton, giving Higgins' hand a good grip. 'Now, mind you come sharp to your time,' continued he, resuming the master. 'I'll have no laggards at my mill. What fines we have, we keep pretty sharply. And the first time I catch you making mischief, off you go. So now you know where you are.'

'Yo' spoke of my wisdom this morning. I reckon I may bring it wi' me; or would yo' rayther have me 'bout my brains?'

' 'Bout your brains, if you use them for meddling with my business; with your brains if you can keep to your own.'

'I shall need a deal o' brains to settle where my business ends and yo's begins.'

'Your business has not begun yet, and mine stands still for me. So good afternoon.'

After this exchange, Higgins remarked later: 'Yon Thornton's good enough to fight wi', but too good for to be cheated.' A strike appeared imminent. Margaret said to Mr Thornton, 'I see two classes dependent on each other in every possible way yet each evidently regarding the interests of the other as opposed to their own; I have never lived in a place before where there were two sets of people always running each other down.'

These were exactly Mrs Gaskell's own feelings when she first went to Manchester from the peace of Knutsford.

North and South was welcomed by the public. The picture it gave of the owners roused none of the resentment of the earlier novel, while it continued to paint the horrors of starvation and misery among the strike-bound families. There was no strike pay in those days.

The other serial, *Cranford,* at once found a wide, popular readership, and remains unique. From her lively memories of childhood days in Knutsford, Mrs Gaskell portrays a small community of elderly ladies who were behind the times even then. Impressions of childhood were now reinforced by the reflections of a mature and sympathetic woman, and the result was a delicately ironic idyll.

The tale is told in the first person by Mary Smith, daughter of a Drumble (Manchester) business man who often visits Cranford and is entertained by the elderly widows and spinsters. She knows all about their poverty, their unconscious snobbery and their kind and generous hearts, and loves them for it all.

The first instalment in *Household Words* began: 'In the first place, Cranford is in possession of the Amazons; all the holders of houses above a certain rent are women. If a married couple come to settle in the town, somehow the gentleman disappears; he is either fairly frightened to death at being the only man in the Cranford evening parties, or he is accounted for by being with his regiment, his ship, or closely engaged in business all the week in the great neighbouring commercial town of Drumble, distant only twenty miles on a railroad. In short, whatever does become of the gentlemen, they are not at Cranford.'

However, a certain Captain Brown arrived with his two daughters. He was not accepted by the ladies for some time, but his good nature and his refusal to feel slighted gradually won over their prejudices, until they even came to take his advice. Miss Betsy Barker's Alderney cow, 'which she looked upon as a daughter' had tumbled into a lime pit and lost her hair. The captain advised the wailing Miss Barker, 'Get her a flannel waistcoat and flannel drawers, ma'am, if you wish to keep her alive. But my advice is, kill the poor creature at once.' 'Miss Betsy Barker dried her eyes and thanked the Captain heartily; she set to work, and by and by all the town turned out to see the Alderney meekly going to her pasture clad in dark grey flannel. I have watched her myself, many a time.'

Miss Pole was the strong-minded spinster: 'Well!' said Miss Pole, sitting down with the decision of a person who has made up her mind as to the nature of life and the world (and such people never tread lightly, or seat themselves without a bump), 'well, Miss Matty, men will be men. Every mother's son of them wishes to be considered Samson and Solomon rolled into one—too strong ever to be beaten or discomfited—too wise ever to be outwitted. If you will notice, they have always foreseen events, though they never tell one for one's warning before the event happens. My father was a man and I know the sex pretty well.'

Here now is a picture of the Honourable Mrs Jamieson, as Elizabeth, as a child, must have seen her: 'The tea-tray was abundantly loaded—I was pleased to see it, I was so hungry; but I was afraid the ladies present might think it vulgarly heaped up. I know they would have done at their own houses; but somehow the heaps disappeared here. I saw Mrs Jamieson eating seed-cake, slowly and considerately, as she did everything; and I was rather surprised, for I knew she had told us on the occasion of her last party, that she never had it in her house, it reminded her so much of scented soap.

She always gave us Savoy biscuits. However, Mrs Jamieson was kindly indulgent to Miss Barker's want of knowledge of the customs of high life; and, to spare her feelings, ate three large pieces of seed-cake, with a placid, ruminating expression of countenance, not unlike a cow's.'

Mrs Gaskell's popularity was almost eclipsed by her next novel, *Ruth* published in 1853. This was a simple story, sympathetically told, but it dealt with a subject taboo of Victorian days—the unmarried mother. Ruth was a young, innocent girl whose lover cruelly deserted her before their child was born. At her darkest hour, she was befriended by a young Nonconformist minister and his sister. Their kindness never faltered, athough they were attacked by many conventionally 'good' people for helping Ruth.

After the baby was born, Ruth found comfort and encouragement in caring for it. She trained as a nurse, and at last became matron of a fever hospital in the same town that had despised her. She became its heroine during an epidemic; her last patient was the man who had deserted her; and she herself caught the fever and died.

Such, briefly, was the theme which shocked and outraged the public, and brought private grief to Mrs Gaskell. She had hoped that her plea for charity would defeat intolerance; many thought that good people, particularly women, should not know social problems much less write about them. She wrote in one letter : 'I think I must be an improper woman without knowing it, I do so manage to shock people.' In another, 'the only comparison I can find for myself is to St Sebastian, tied to a tree to be shot at with arrows'.

Yet, although *general* opinion was that 'it was an unfit subject for fiction', many enlightened people realised its importance at the time. Among them were Dickens and Charles Kingsley, Florence Nightingale and Mrs Browning, who interwove a similar theme in her poem-novel *Aurora Leigh*. Charlotte Brontë, whom Mrs Gaskell had told about the story before its publication, was very appreciative but protested : 'Why should she [Ruth] die? Why are we to shut up the book weeping? . . . And yet you must follow the impulse of your own inspiration.'

George Eliot, while admiring the novel, shrewdly commented that it would not become a great classic of fiction since the author loved dramatic effects too much, and was impatient with the half-tints of real life. George Eliot's fine novel with the same theme,

Adam Bede, written some years later, avoids those mistakes. Forgotten today, *Ruth,* was a courageous venture into a new field for women writers. There were indeed some good reviews at the time and Mrs Gaskell was not crushed for long, as this extract from a letter to a friend shows :

'The *North British Review* has a *delicious* review of *Ruth* in it. Who the deuce could have written it? It is so truly religious it makes me swear with delight. I think it is one of the Christian Socialists, but I can't make out which. I must get William to find out.'

Two other novels by this busy woman must be briefly mentioned, neither of which, however, presented any social problems. *Sylvia's Lovers* is a gloomy melodramatic tale of Whitby in Yorkshire and its surroundings in the days of smugglers and press-gangs. 'It is the saddest story I have ever written,' said its author, and, indeed, except for some of the minor characters, the well-drawn farmers, shopkeepers and fishermen, there is little to lighten the tragedy of Sylvia and her two sailor lovers.

Wives and Daughters, her last book, not completely finished at her death, is a pleasant, slow-moving domestic tale, in the *Cranford* vein. It has some entertaining, well-contrasted characters and the whole book is satisfying to read.

Mrs Gaskell once said that if any of her work was likely to last, it would be *Cranford.* She was right. But she left one other outstanding achievement, her *Life of Charlotte Brontë,* begun four months after Charlotte's death at the request of Mr Brontë himself. It was a great honour and responsibility, and Mrs Gaskell's task was on the whole well done. But in her zeal to do justice to her great friend she made several errors of judgment which upset people still alive. When she came home from a holiday in Italy to find herself once more in hot water, she at once had public apologies made, and the noise slowly subsided.

Mrs Gaskell, by nature and temperament, did not reach the same heights and depths as Charlotte Brontë. But she brought a generous admiration and sympathy to her writing, and combined it with the information given by Charlotte's closest friends. Her biography is the foundation of the host of books that have been written about the Brontë family ever since.

Elizabeth Gaskell had tucked away the money she was paid for *Wives and Daughters.* Her husband this time did not see a penny of it. She used it to buy a house in a Hampshire village as a present for him when he should be ready to retire.

She and her family were staying in the house, when one day in 1865 she died suddenly, sitting in the garden. She was fifty-five. During her life she had done much and made a valuable contribution to the woman's view of the contemporary scene.

TEN

Charlotte Brontë

IT IS IMPOSSIBLE to write of Charlotte Brontë separately from the rest of her family. She and her sisters, Emily and Anne, and to some extent her brother Branwell, had a unity of thought and feeling that was far more deep and powerful than most bonds of family affection. Mrs Gaskell, when writing the life of Charlotte, said, 'The family with whom I now have to do shot their roots down deeper than I can penetrate. I cannot measure them; much less is it for me to judge them.' And again, 'They were all in all to each other. I do not suppose that there ever was a family more tenderly bound to each other.'

The story of this brilliant but short-lived family has fascinated thousands of ordinary men and women ever since they died. Their home, the famous Parsonage at Haworth in Yorkshire, has become a museum in their honour and a place of pilgrimage, probably second only to Stratford-upon-Avon. Countless books and several plays have been written about them, yet the secret of their hold on the public imagination has never been fully revealed.

The word 'imagination' is the key word in approaching them. They lived life on two levels, the ordinary day to day existence, often monotonous and, for the girls, full of domestic duties, and then the secret, romantic life where their passionate loves and hates had full play.

As children, unknown to their elders, they had created worlds of their own of which they wrote in small booklets in tiny handwriting. Charlotte and Branwell worked together in their tales of the *Angrians*, while Emily and Anne produced the adventures of the *Gondals.* These came to light for the first time after they had all died. Fortunately for the world, they continued to write all their lives and realised that they had something within them which demanded an outlet and a response from readers.

They were the children of the Reverend Patrick Brontë (originally 'Brunty'), an Irishman of humble origins, and his wife Maria, a member of a Cornish Methodist family. Mr Brontë was rather eccentric even in the early days of his marriage and his oddities increased with age. His gentle wife bore him six children, one a boy, during the time they lived in several Yorkshire parishes. Charlotte and her sisters were born at Thornton, near Bradford.

But it is with Haworth, a village on the edge of the moors near Keighley in the West Riding of Yorkshire, that the family is associated. Mr Brontë was appointed to the living when they were very young, and they stayed there for the rest of their lives. It is very obvious from their writings, particularly those of Emily, that they were much influenced by the surrounding countryside. The wild and magnificent stretches of moorland, the great rocks and rushing falls of water, appealed strongly to their romantic imaginations and they used and appreciated this natural grandeur as if native to it. But they were not Yorkshire people and their inheritance—Irish and Cornish—must be remembered when their genius is considered.

Mrs Brontë, a gifted and well-read woman, was very delicate and did not live long in Haworth Parsonage. She was seriously ill for some time before her death and the six little children grew unnaturally quiet and clung closely together in fear. After their mother died, her sister, Miss Branwell, came from Cornwall to take charge of the household. She was very kind but did not win the confidence of the strange little family, although they were always obedient to her.

Mr Brontë spent much time alone and preferred to have his meals apart from the family. Miss Branwell had her own room and the children spent most of their time in a small upstairs room where they lived an absorbing, secret life of their own. The Parsonage is surrounded on three sides by the ancient churchyard and the children could not play out of doors. When, later, Charlotte was at school, another pupil noticed that she had no idea how to play with a ball. But Charlotte's eyesight was always poor, so that may help explain her inability. But from an early age the children would go off, hand in hand, to enjoy the freedom of the moors, to watch the clouds and feel the wind and lie in the heather.

With the beginning of schooldays came trouble. Mr Brontë,

whose stipend was barely enough to keep them, decided to send the older girls to a boarding school where the fees were low. This was the School for the Daughters of the Clergy at Cowan Bridge, near Kirby Lonsdale. Here, the extremely sensitive little girls, who had never had the chance to meet other children, were utterly miserable. The school was not well run, its position was unhealthy, the food was badly cooked and the discipline was far too harsh.

Maria Brontë, the eldest, became ill, and her condition rapidly worsened. Tragically, she died. As if this were not enough, the next sister died of a similar fever soon afterwards. Charlotte never outgrew the effect of this double tragedy. The death of her sisters at school and the callousness of the staff were to cause her anger and misery for the rest of her life. Some of that anger went into her account of Lowood School and its founder in *Jane Eyre*. In the book the schoolgirl, Helen Burns, is a portrait of her sister Maria and Miss Scatchard represents the cruel mistress who treated the poor child so badly. Later on the Cowan Bridge school did improve and Charlotte regretted that she had let her own feelings colour her picture of 'Lowood' so far.

Charlotte and Emily, who had been taken home by their father after the death of their sisters, returned to school. Charlotte was determined that, whatever her feelings, she would have all the education she could get. They stayed another year, but were then taken away because the place was unhealthily damp.

At home, for some time they continued to write, to read biography, history and poetry and to listen to conversation between their father and some of his men parishioners. They were very precocious, eager to lap up all kinds of information. They were particularly fascinated by politics, were violently Tory, and regarded the Duke of Wellington as their greatest hero. They kept in touch with what went on in the village through spending much time in the kitchen of their faithful servant Tabitha. Tabby, as they called her, was devoted to them, and so was the young woman from the village who came to help Tabby as she grew older. The warmth of Tabby's kitchen was something they all enjoyed.

In her early teens, Charlotte was small, neat and brown-haired, and though short-sighted her brown eyes were very expressive of her feelings. She looked a little prim in her old-fashioned clothes and her manner was that of someone with too much responsibility and old before her time. She was always shy, whereas Emily was proud and reserved and had no wish to make friends, caring for no one except her sisters.

With a gentler nature, Charlotte was able to spend some happy years at their second school at Roe Head, near Huddersfield. There, under a kind headmistress who later became a close friend, she eagerly devoted herself to learning, improved her gift for drawing and made two life-long friends, Mary Taylor and Ellen Nussey. Both these, especially Ellen, gave much information about Charlotte to Mrs Gaskell, her biographer. Charlotte was a welcome visitor in their homes and always kept in touch with them, though Miss Taylor eventually went to live in New Zealand and did not keep many of Charlotte's letters.

After leaving school Charlotte stayed at home for a time. She combined her cooking and other domestic duties with reading— both she and Emily could read as they cooked. Often, they took eight-mile walks to Keighley and back to borrow library books and went for long walks and talks on the moors.

Both Charlotte and Emily had decided to teach in order to earn a living, but both hated the idea of being governesses in a private family. In 1835 Charlotte returned to Roe Head as a teacher and Emily as a pupil. Emily managed to stay three months before being overcome by homesickness, not so much for the Parsonage as for solitude and the moors. She always seemed to be stifled by any kind of routine and discipline, however gentle. As Mrs Gaskell wrote : 'Emily was never happy nor well but on the sweeping moors that gathered round her home.'

At least, however, she looked after her father and her aunt, so that Charlotte was fairly easy in her mind while away from home. Charlotte's nerves were always tense and her fears innumerable; even a sudden loud noise would terrify her and she hated being in darkness, sitting rigid in the grip of terror. She had a deep religious faith yet had no hope of ordinary comfort or happiness. Later events certainly did little to encourage her, except her success as a writer.

When she left Roe Head she began to look for a place as a governess. By now, she had changed her idea about it : 'I see everything *couleur de rose* and am strongly inclined to dance a jig, if I knew how . . . A woman of the name of Mrs B. it seems, wants a teacher. I wish she would have me; and I have written to Miss W. to tell her so. Verily, it is a delightful thing to live here at home, at full liberty to do just what one pleases. But I recollect some scrubby old fable about grasshoppers and ants, by a scrubby old knave y-clept [called] Aesop; the grasshopper sang all the summer and starved all the winter.'

Twice Charlotte tried to be a governess but failed each time. Her young sister Anne had the same trouble, and for the same reason: they did not understand children. Their own childhood was unreal, and they resented being dependent on the goodwill of others. Being, by nature, proud they often saw insult where none was intended. It is true that the position of a governess was, in many households, an unenviable one. They were often treated with only the barest politeness by their employers and with insolence by children and servants.

Charlotte, however, does not seem to have been in an unpleasant household but she was quick to imagine slights and was very unhappy. When, years later, she stayed at Mrs Gaskell's home in Manchester she could hardly believe that her four little daughters were perfectly ordinary children because they were so well-behaved and delightful. They won her heart, but perhaps they had been luckier in their upbringing than Charlotte's former pupils.

In *Vilette*, written years afterwards, she gave vent, not for the first time, to her feelings about being a governess: 'I could teach; I could give lessons; but to be either a private governess or a companion was unnatural to me. Rather than fill the former post in any great house, I would deliberately have taken a housemaid's place, bought a strong pair of gloves, swept bedrooms and staircases and cleaned stoves and locks in peace and independence. Rather than be a companion, I would have made shirts and starved.'

The reference to shirt-making is interesting, as it was one of the worst-paid of all types of work, and known as 'sweated labour'. In *The Song of the Shirt* Thomas Hood had made a plea for these unhappy workers.

Having at last agreed that they could never endure the lives of governesses, Charlotte and Emily decided that their aim should be to open a school at the Parsonage for a few boarders. First they must prepare themselves for the task and fortunately for them their aunt was interested in the plan. She agreed to give them £100 to go to a school in Brussels to perfect their French and also learn German. So in 1842 they ventured into the unknown. Another extract from *Vilette* gives a clear picture of the mind of its heroine, Lucy Snowe, as she arrived friendless in France; the words were surely based on Charlotte's memories of her own feelings on arriving in Belgium:

'The sky was monotonously grey; the atmosphere was stagnant and humid; yet amid all these deadening influences my fancy budded fresh and my heart basked in sunshine. These feelings, however, were well kept in check by the secret but ceaseless consciousness of anxiety lying in wait on enjoyment, like a tiger crouched in the jungle. The breathing of that beast of prey was in my ears always, his fierce heart panted close against mine; he never stirred in his lair but I felt him. I knew he waited only for sundown to bound ravenous from his ambush.'

Such was Charlotte's imaginative treatment of a new experience.

The school they went to in Brussels was kept by Madame Héger, helped by her husband. There the two sisters attracted attention not only for their odd assortment of clothes and complete dependence on each other, but also for the extraordinary talents they revealed. M. Héger, a wise and kindly man, saw their great possibilities. He was particularly amazed by Emily's genius; her poetic and imaginative gifts were allied with a clear logical mind which made her skilful in argument. She was, however, completely self-reliant and self-willed and it was impossible to deflect her from an idea or purpose once her mind was made up. It had been true of her as a child and, sadly, it remained true even in the last months before her death at twenty-nine.

Before their stay in Brussels ended, Miss Branwell died and the sisters travelled at once to Haworth. They were prepared to stay at home, but a very kind letter from M. Héger invited Charlotte to return to the school as a teacher of English for a year. In this way she would have money to pay for the rest of her lessons. It was agreed that she should go, and that Emily would look after their father, whose eyesight was failing and who was having to find extra money to pay a curate to help him in the parish.

In Brussels Charlotte found life lonely and depressing. She missed Emily dreadfully, feeling ill most of the time and cold all the time. At first, she had difficulty keeping class discipline, but she refused all help from the Hégers. She wrote to a friend : 'I hope I am thankful; and if I could always keep up my spirits, and never feel lonely or long for companionship or friendship, or whatever they call it, I should do very well.'

Her depression persisted both during the school terms and the holidays, when she stayed in the school to continue her German studies. She could not sleep and was worried about her father's health and about her brother, Branwell, who was already causing the family anxiety by his wildness and heavy drinking bouts. She disliked Mme. Héger and the Roman Catholic atmosphere at the school, for she was an uncompromising, even intolerant, Anglican herself. But gradually her Belgian pupils responded to her and when she left Brussels early in 1844 she realised that they were sincerely sorry to see her go. Charlotte could never believe that anyone, except her sisters, could have any affection for her. She doubted if people even *liked* her. Animals, especially the timid ones, were her only real friends.

Unfortunately, while at the school, Charlotte had found herself falling in love with M. Héger, who had always treated her with great kindness and understanding. But he had kept his distance. He was careful to regard her as a clever, even brilliant young woman who had benefited by his teaching and encouragement. Charlotte's manner was always calm and self-contained but her passionate feelings were revealed in a series of letters she wrote from Haworth to M. Héger, who left them unanswered. This sad story came to light some years after her death when four of her letters were found in a box of Mme Héger. It is also used by Charlotte, as was so much of her own experience, in the story of Lucy Snowe and M. Paul Emanuel in *Vilette*.

As well as her own secret troubles, there was much at home to distress Charlotte. She and Emily still hoped to start a school and drew up a prospectus and a small advertisement. But no one it seems wanted to send their daughters to bleak, remote Haworth. Mr Brontë's health grew worse with his blindness, and Branwell's intemperance and drug-taking was nearing a climax. This brilliant and handsome young man, who had many signs of genius and was his father's pride and delight, had a fatal streak of moral weakness.

He had got into the habit of drinking at The Black Bull in Haworth and was too lazy to work in the various posts that were found for him. When his youngest sister, Anne, was governess for a short time to a family's girls, Branwell went to tutor the boys. The result was that he became infatuated with the wife of his employer and could not believe that she did not share his passion. There are various versions of the story and it is not clear how far the lady had encouraged him or how cruelly she threw him out.

The fact remains that after that Branwell devoted himself to drink and drugs. But his family never stopped loving or looking after him. Mr Brontë stayed up with him night after night as he grappled with delirium and remorse. The girls nursed him and wept over his tragedy and the shame in which it involved the family. They even managed to scrape together the money to pay his debts. This continued for some years. Charlotte sometimes read aloud to her father, but her own eyesight was failing. Emily had developed a racking cough which troubled her more and more and they all suffered miserably from the long cold winters.

The year 1845 was an important one for the Brontë sisters. They had all at various times written poetry and when Charlotte accidentally discovered some of Emily's work she managed to persuade her to try to have them published, together with some by Anne and herself. They were sure that if it was known they were women their work would have little chance of publication so they chose for themselves the non-committal names of Currer (Charlotte), Ellis (Emily) and Acton (Anne) Bell.

Charlotte dealt with all the necessary business and after some refusals found a publisher willing to publish the poems at the author's own expense. Charlotte anxiously enquired about costs and then paid immediately. The poems, except those by Emily, which were praised by the critics, went almost unnoticed and the 'Messrs Bell' were disappointed but not beaten.

As well as poetry, each sister had also written a novel. Emily's was *Wuthering Heights*, Anne had written the story of the trials of a governess in *Agnes Grey* and Charlotte's first work was *The Professor*. These were sent to many publishers and always returned unwanted. But even with these disappointments Charlotte began her second novel, telling her sisters : 'I will show you a heroine as plain and small as myself, who shall be as interesting as any of yours.' This she did in *Jane Eyre*.

In 1847 both *Wuthering Heights* and *Agnes Grey* found a publisher. *The Professor*, however, was declined by the firm of Smith, Elder. But they were so courteous about it that Charlotte ventured to tell them that Currer Bell had nearly finished another, more exciting novel, which he hoped might be favourably received. So *Jane Eyre* was sent to the publishers in August and came out in October, some time before *Wuthering Heights* and *Agnes Grey*.

Mr Smith of Smith, Elder and Company, was so greatly impressed by *Jane Eyre* that he took a peronal interest in the critical reviews and the reactions of famous literary men to it. He also sent all comments and reviews to Mr Currer Bell at Haworth.

Nothing had been said to Mr Brontë until the novel actually appeared. Charlotte then told him and left him with a copy of the book. Shortly before this he had had a successful operation for cataract, and so could read the book for himself. He appeared at tea-time, remarking : 'Girls, do you know Charlotte has been writing a book, and it is much better than likely?'

Other readers were more generous with praise and there was

much speculation about the author of this powerful romantic drama which Mrs Gaskell later called : 'a work which the great flood of public opinion has lifted up from the obscurity in which it first appeared, and laid, high and safe, on the everlasting hills of fame.'

The book, like Charlotte Brontë's other novels, is based largely on her own experiences, transmuted by her imagination into vivid life. *Jane Eyre* is told in the first person, as befits the work of so subjective a writer. It tells the adventures of a plain, insignificant governess, who is transformed by her love for her darkly romantic employer, Mr Rochester. She is probably the secret woman that lay within Charlotte herself, but only in her novels could that woman struggle free. Jane in love can be demure or sparkling, tender or fierce, tragic or gay as occasion arises. *Jane Eyre* is an exciting, almost melodramatic story and, after much suffering, a happy ending.

It is interesting that George Henry Lewes, the writer and critic, of whom more will be said in the account of George Eliot, wrote highly appreciative reviews of *Jane Eyre*. However, he wrote to its author privately, suggesting that much as he admired the work, he felt that there were rather too many 'situations' and too much melodrama. He even suggested that Currer Bell might profit by reading Jane Austen. Part of Charlotte's reply runs thus :

'When authors write best, or, at least, most fluently, an influence seems to waken in them, which becomes their master—which will have its own way—putting out of view all behests but its own ... dictating certain words and insisting on their being used, whether vehement or measured in their nature ... Is it not so? And should we try to counteract that influence? Can we indeed counteract it?'

And, again, 'Why do you like Miss Austen so very much? I am puzzled on that point. What induced you to say that you would have rather written *Pride and Prejudice* or *Tom Jones* than any of the Waverley novels?'

In his reply, Lewes tried to explain his point, but she retaliated : 'Miss Austen being, as you say, without sentiment, without *poetry*, maybe *is* sensible, real (more real than true), but she cannot be great. I submit to your anger, which I have now excited (for have I not questioned the perfection of your darling?); the storm may pass over me. Nevertheless, I will, when I can (I do not know when that will be as I have no access to a circulating library), diligently peruse all Miss Austen's works, as you recommend.'

She did not become a convert to Jane Austen, but she was obviously stimulated and enjoyed appreciation and criticism like that of Lewes. Other reviewers were not so kind; *Jane Eyre* was even described as 'wicked' by the responsible *Quarterly Review*. It was too outspoken for some, and the men in the book did not show a 'proper respect' for women. Moreover, it was actually 'coarse' in places! Charlotte was not too worried; she had other anxieties on her mind. She wrote : 'It is my nature, when left alone, to struggle on with a certain perseverance and I believe God will help me.'

Mrs Gaskell, always the champion of the Brontës, wrote : 'It is possible that it would have been better to have described only good and pleasant people, doing only good and pleasant things (in which case they could hardly have written at any time) : all I say is, that never, I believe, did women, possessed of such wonderful gifts, exercise them with a fuller feeling of responsibility for their use.'

When at last *Wuthering Heights* and *Agnes Grey* were published they were not very well received and Charlotte's pleasure in her own success was lessened by her sorrow that Emily's genius should be unrecognised. Indeed it was not until some years after her death that people began to realise that her book was something unique.

When it was published it was suggested by some critics that it, and *Agnes Grey*, could only be inferior works by the author of *Jane Eyre*. That decided Charlotte. She and Anne (the author of *Agnes Grey* and later of *The Tenant of Wildfell Hall*) would go to London to see Mr Smith, the publisher, and in secret let him know their real identity.

The two sisters with their small pieces of luggage walked down to Keighley station in a violent thunderstorm and arrived in London bedraggled and tired, but not dismayed. They went to stay at the same rather odd little hotel in which they had put up for the night before going to Brussels.

When they arrived, unheralded, in Mr Smith's room he could hardly believe that the two quiet ladies were indeed the 'Messrs Bell', one of them the famous author of *Jane Eyre*. He treated them with all the honour in his power and invited them as his guests to his London home, but they decided to stay at their hotel. He insisted that they must come to his home and meet some of the famous people who would love to meet such a celebrated novelist. They hesitatingly agreed to go with Mr and Mrs Smith to the opera that night and returned to their hotel.

Charlotte, having had no sleep at all the previous night and having caught a bad chill from her soaking in the storm was very

ill and in great pain for some hours. But fortunately, she threw
off the worst of it, and felt that they *must* go to the opera to show
good manners.

For a weekend they were royally entertained. No one seemed to
notice their shabby clothes and everyone was impressed by Charlotte's quiet assurance. They liked her genuine interest in the
opinions of others and her real eloquence whether in praise or
criticism of the books that were discussed. In fact, the shy Charlotte was a social success!

They returned to Haworth, tired out but happy, loaded down
with books from Mr Smith who from now on posted such gifts
regularly to Haworth.

But 1848 was not only a year of triumph for Charlotte. It was
the time of her greatest sorrow. Branwell's wretched life at last
came to an end. He was only thirty. Emily was getting rapidly
worse and seemed to keep going only by frightening willpower. She
coughed incessantly and was weakened by breathlessness. But she
would let no one speak of her health or try to help her. She refused
to see a doctor until it was too late. She died just before Christmas,
causing Charlotte a loss from which she never recovered.

To Ellen Nussey she wrote: 'Your friendship is some comfort to
me. I am thankful for it. I see few lights through the darkness of
the present time, but amongst them the constancy of a kind heart
attached to me is one of the most cheering and serene.' And again:
'Emily is nowhere here now; her wasted mortal remains are
taken out of the house ... Well, the loss is ours, not hers, and
some sad comfort I take, as I hear the wind blow and feel the
cutting edge of the frost, in knowing that the elements bring her
no more suffering. Their severity cannot reach her grave; her
fever is quieted; her restlessness soothed; her deep, hollow cough
is hushed for ever; we do not hear it in the night nor listen for it
in the morning. We have not the conflict of the strangely strong
spirit and the fragile frame before us—relentless conflict, once seen,
never to be forgotten. A dreary calm reigns round us, in the midst
of which we seek resignation ... So I will not now ask why Emily
was torn from us in the fullness of our attachment, rooted up in
the prime of her own days, in the promise of her powers; why her
existence now lies like a field of green corn trodden down, like a
tree in full bearing struck at the root. I will only say, sweet is
rest after labour and calm after tempest, and repeat again and
again that Emily knows that now.'

The same dreadful consumptive fever that had killed Emily

was steadily sapping the life of Anne, who had never been robust. Gently and gratefully she accepted the help that Charlotte and old Tabby could give her. She had once visited Scarborough and now longed again for the sea. Charlotte managed to arrange that she and a friend should take Anne again to Scarborough in late May 1849. This was done, but a few days after their arrival Anne's gentle life ended and she was buried in the cliff-top graveyard of Scarborough parish church.

Charlotte knew the depths of loneliness. Ever since childhood, the sisters used to meet at nine o'clock every evening to talk about their writing, pacing round the room. Now there was only Charlotte, who paced alone. She kept this habit, as Mrs Gaskell heard when she stayed at the Parsonage and, from her room, listened to the steady tread below.

Charlotte had already begun her next book before Emily's death. She continued it, despite her misery, and into it went her picture of Emily as she might have been if life had been kind to her. Shirley Keeldar, heroine of *Shirley* has many of Emily's characteristics, including a fierce and passionate love of animals. Shirley's dog 'Tartar' is very like Emily Brontë's 'Keeper', whose savage spirit she tamed to be obedient to her.

Charlotte's friend Ellen Nussey also went into the book, as Shirley's friend Caroline Helston. But it is Charlotte's own views they express in this conversation : 'Caroline says, "Shirley, men and women are so different; they are in such a different position. Women have so few things to think about—men so many. Much of what cheers your life may be dependent on him, while not a feeling or interest of moment in his eyes may have reference to you." And again : "Caroline," demanded Miss Keeldar abruptly, "don't you wish you had a profession or trade?"

' "I wish it fifty times a day. As it is, I often wonder what I came into the world for. I long to have something absorbing and compulsory to fill my head and hands and to occupy my thoughts."

' "Can labour alone make a human being happy?"

' "No, but it can give varieties of pain, and prevent us from breaking our hearts with a single tyrant master torture. Besides, successful labour has its recompense; a vacant, weary, lonely, hopeless life has none." '

In that belief Charlotte continued to write. The theme of *Shirley* was the troubles of an earlier time and the subject was suggested by a memory of her schooldays at Roe House. The Headmistress, Miss Wooler, had told her pupils of the troubles that had broken out in that very district of Yorkshire when machinery was first introduced in the mills in 1812. The 'Luddites', named after their leader, had wrecked the machines and burned down some of the mills. Mr Brontë confirmed all this from his own recollections of his early parishes in the district. Charlotte borrowed copies of the *Leeds Mercury* newspaper for the years 1812–4 to see just what had happened. Although she was using an earlier setting and story, many of the characters were suggested by people she knew. Many later recognised themselves in the book. Of the three curates she described—with great candour and some severity—the one to whom she was kindest was the one who was to figure later in her own life. All three had originally helped her father at Haworth.

Her publisher was anxious that *Shirley* should repeat the success of *Jane Eyre*. Charlotte insisted, however, that she must write it entirely in her own way : 'The two human beings who understood me, and whom I understood, are gone; I have some that love me yet, and whom I love, without expecting, or having a right to expect, that they shall perfectly understand me ... The faculty of imagination lifted me when I was sinking, three months ago; its active exercise has kept my head above water since; its results cheer me now, for I feel they have enabled me to give pleasure to others. I am thankful to God, who gave me the faculty; and it is for me a part of my religion to defend this gift, and to profit by its possession.'

The publisher's delight with *Shirley* encouraged her for she had feared she would disappoint the public with a second book. It was after enjoying *Shirley* that Mrs Gaskell first wrote to Charlotte and sent her a copy of her own *Mary Barton*. Thus began a friendship which ripened over the years. They met for the first time at the home of a mutual friend in the Lake District.

The welcome given to *Shirley* helped Charlotte in her difficult life at home. Tabby had become a permanent invalid and needed tender nursing. Mr Brontë was feeble and difficult in many ways, and the house had to be immaculately kept to satisfy Charlotte's love of cleanliness and neatness. She began to feel ill herself and decided that, when she could, she would take a coach and see a doctor in London.

Gradually the identity of Currer Bell was becoming known. This was largely through the acumen of a Yorkshire businessman who declared that none but a woman, and one who knew Yorkshire's West Riding well, could possibly have written *Shirley*. So the great

news broke at Haworth and Charlotte was amused and pleased at
its reception. She wrote :

'Martha (the young maid) came in yesterday, puffing and blow-
ing and much excited. "I've heard sich news!" she began.

' "What about?"

' "Please, ma'am, you've been and written two books—the grand-
est books that ever was seen. My father has heard of it at Halifax
and Mr G.T. and Mr G. and Mr M. at Bradford; and they are
going to have a meeting at the Mechanics' Institute, and to settle
about ordering them!"

' "Hold your tongue, Martha, and be off." '

She goes on : 'Heaven help, keep and deliver me!—the Haworth
people have been making great fools of themselves about *Shirley*.'

When Charlotte visited London she stayed with the Smiths as
she was to do on later occasions. By this time she was becoming
known as Miss Brontë and enjoyed meeting various celebrities.
She was specially glad to meet Harriet Martineau, the deaf but
discriminating writer and critic, whose social and political writings
were admired by Charlotte. The two became friends and Charlotte
paid a visit to Miss Martineau's house near Windermere where
she met Mrs Gaskell.

William Makepeace Thackeray was another whom Charlotte
met with real pleasure. He thought so highly of her as a novelist
that his appreciation once caused her much embarrassment. She
went, at his invitation, to hear him lecture and when he had
finished he came straight down to her as she sat at the front and
asked her what she had thought of it. As she and her friend rose
from their chairs to leave they saw that almost the entire audience
had lined the aisle down which she must pass to do her honour.
This terrified poor Charlotte. Thackeray's action in publicly seeking
her opinion was used in a similar episode in her last novel, *Vilette,*
between the professor, Paul Emanuel, and Lucy Snowe.

On one London visit Charlotte watched a theatre performance
by the great tragic actress Rachel. Her reactions, as might be
expected, were passionate : 'a wonderful sight—terrible as if the
earth had cracked deep at your feet, and revealed a glimpse of hell.
I shall never forget it. She made me shudder to the marrow of my
bones; in her some fiend has certainly taken up an incarnate home.
She is not a woman; she is a snake . . .'

Similarly, in *Vilette,* when her heroine, Lucy, describes a tragic
actress it is really Charlotte's own reactions to the power of imagination that are being expressed : 'The strong magnetism of genius

drew my heart out of its wonted orbit, the sunflower turned from the south to a fierce light—not solar—a rushing, red, cometary light—hot on vision and to sensation. I had seen acting before, but never anything like this; never anything which astonished Hope and hushed Desire; which outstripped Impulse and paled Conception; which, instead of merely irritating imagination with the thought of what *might* be done, at the same time fevering the nerves because it was *not* done, disclosed power like a deep, swollen, winter river, thundering in cataract, and bearing the soul, like a leaf, on the steep and steely sweep of its descent.'

In spite of her visits to London and the occasional ones to her two old friends, Charlotte continued to be depressed and nerveracked at home. It was even worse in the long winter nights when she could not sleep. Her father and the servants were in bed by eight o'clock and she herself could do nothing, since her eyes were too weak for reading or sewing. High winds moaning on the moors always distressed her and her thoughts were gloomy as she remembered the days in Brussels and her unrequited love. She knew that only in writing could she find any kind of relief, and *Vilette* was written in a mood of dark depression.

She wrote of it : 'I cannot write books handling the topics of the day; it is of no use trying. Nor can I write a book for its moral. Nor can I take up a philanthropic scheme, though I honour philanthropy, and voluntarily and sincerely veil my face before such a mighty subject as is handled in Mrs Beecher Stowe's work, *Uncle Tom's Cabin*. To manage these great matters rightly, they must be long and practically studied—their bearings known intimately and their evils felt genuinely.'

Vilette describes the adventures in France of Lucy Snowe. Lucy was intended by the author to be cold and reserved, but seen—in her experiences—to be full of weaknesses and even tinged with morbidity. Her adventures are not unlike those of Charlotte in Brussels and the tale, like *Jane Eyre,* is told in the first person.

It must have been some relief to Charlotte to write, in the person of Lucy, some of her own fears, hopes and disappointments, for Lucy, like Charlotte, loved her professor. But Lucy's love was returned by the autocratic Paul Emanuel, a character in many ways resembling Mr Rochester in *Jane Eyre.* Mr Brontë begged Charlotte to give *Vilette* a happy ending. Charlotte was reluctant to do so, but compromised with an ambiguous one, beautifully expressed and leaving thoughtful readers in no doubt of her true intention.

By way of contrast, *Vilette* has more than one example of her sense of humour. Here is Lucy's description of a concert given in the presence of royalty : 'Following the white muslin pianistes came a fine, full-grown sulky lady in white satin. Her singing just affected me like the tricks of a conjuror; I wondered how she did it—how she made her voice run up and down, and cut such marvellous capers, but a simple scotch melody, played by a rude street minstrel, has often moved me more deeply.

'Afterwards stepped forth a gentleman who, bending his body a good deal in the direction of the King and Queen, and frequently approaching his white-gloved hand to the region of his heart, vented a bitter outcry against a certain "fausse Isabelle". I thought he seemed especially to solicit the Queen's sympathy, but unless I am egregiously mistaken, her Majesty lent her attention rather with the calm of courtesy than the earnestness of interest. This gentleman's state of mind was very harrowing and I was glad when he wound up his musical exposition of the same.'

This is certainly an unusual vein for Charlotte Brontë in her novels, although flashes of fun are seen in many of her letters.

When in 1853 *Vilette* was ready for publication, Charlotte travelled to London and found that Mrs Gaskell's *Ruth* was just about to be published, also by Smith, Elder. She at once asked that her own novel should wait until *Ruth* was properly launched. She must not risk spoiling the chances of Mrs Gaskell's work. Charlotte wrote, 'there is a goodness, a philanthropic purpose, a social use in it to which *Vilette* cannot, for an instant, pretend.'

About this time she and Mrs Gaskell began to visit each other and each wrote appreciatively of the other's home and hospitality. Mrs Gaskell, as she walked over the moorlands at Haworth, had no idea that she would soon be invited to write *The Life of Charlotte Brontë*.

Twice before Charlotte had received proposals of marriage but had never taken them seriously. Of marriage she once wrote : 'If ever I marry, it must be in that light of adoration that I will regard my husband . . . I could not sit all day long making a grave face before my husband. I would laugh and satirise and say whatever came into my head first. And if he were a clever man, and loved me, the whole world, weighed in the balance against his smallest wish, should be as light as air.' Shirley, in the novel of that name, had prided herself on doing all that a man could do; she was shrewd and independent, but when once she was in love she gladly gave up all that hard-won independence.

The Reverend Arthur Nicholls, who had been curate to Mr Brontë for some years, had loved Charlotte for a long while but feared that his love would not be returned. He was grave and serious-minded and at last found the courage to ask Charlotte to marry him. She consulted her father who was horrified at the idea of Charlotte's marrying and leaving him alone. So, although she would gladly have accepted the offer, she refused it and Mr Nicholls left the parish. But during the year that followed Charlotte, encouraged by her friend, Miss Wooler, gradually persuaded Mr Brontë that her marriage need not interfere with his comfort. If they married Mr Nicholls could return to his curacy and they would live at the Parsonage and continue to look after Mr Brontë.

So it was agreed, and in 1854 Miss Wooler and Miss Nussey were invited to Charlotte's wedding. On the wedding day Mr Brontë suddenly refused to come to the ceremony. This was a sad blow to Charlotte. Instead, Miss Wooler gave the bride away and the villagers packed the church to the doors, for Miss Brontë, though shy, had always been very good to them, especially in times of illness and sorrow.

The wedding day was followed by a honeymoon in Ireland, among Mr Nicholls' relatives. The new Mr and Mrs Nicholls returned to Haworth full of hope and zeal. But in March 1855, after only eight months of married happiness, Charlotte died.

Mr Nicholls stayed on at Haworth and he and old Mr Brontë lived on in uneasy companionship, with only their love of Charlotte as a bond between them.

To that household, four months later, came Mrs Gaskell at Mr Brontë's request to begin collecting the material needed for the biography of her friend. Mr Brontë was eager for his daughter's fame to be widely known, but Mr Nicholls cared little for her fame and only mourned his lost wife.

Charlotte Brontë was a unique story-teller. The incidents in the stories are exciting and told in thrilling language; though few in number the characters are very fully drawn, there is great depth of emotion, and passions run high and swift. She creates a vivid atmosphere in both outdoor and indoor scenes, which are always in the same key as the events to which they are a background. Most readers of any of the three great novels become so enthralled that they cannot be drawn away until they have come to the last page, and closed the covers. Such is her magnetic power as a writer.

ELEVEN
George Eliot

GEORGE ELIOT was born in 1819. She added a new dimension to the novel, developing and enlarging the work done by earlier women novelists. They had produced well-constructed, interesting plots, excellent portrayals of character, and stories with convincing and varied backgrounds. The novels of the Brontë sisters also had great intensity of feeling and a powerful sense of atmosphere.

George Eliot's work uses all these things in varying degrees, but she brought an intellectual approach to her tales and their characters. Since she did not begin novel-writing until she was nearly forty, she had had time to observe her fellow humans and to develop a firm philosophy of life. Her own nature was serious and there is purpose, even urgency, in all her work. In each novel she shows that every action brings its own result—for good or ill. Although the wages of sin are forcefully depicted there is nearly always an understanding and tolerance for the sinner. The sometime unpalatable truths she illustrates are made acceptable by the complete naturalness of the characters and the author's wholly delightful and sometimes unexpected sense of humour. This is shown particularly in the characterisation of the many background figures. These people, whether rural or urban, though not part of the main theme, supply comment upon it, rather like the chorus in the ancient Greek dramas.

Unlike Charlotte Brontë, who used very few characters and identified herself completely with some of them, George Eliot is the detached and sympathetic observer. She sees forces set in motion and knows what their outcome must be. Her canvas is broad and well-filled. The main characters are shaped and slowly developed by their experiences while the static or background ones add richness and variety to the setting.

Her best work is a blend of imaginative insight and sound reason. Sometimes, however, her interest in an abstract idea, a special problem or a particular period of history takes up too much time and space and the result is tedious. For this reason, *Romola* (set in medieval Florence) and *Daniel Deronda* (Jewish and Zionist plans and problems) have never been so popular as *The Mill on the Floss, Silas Marner* and *Middlemarch*. In these the characters are timeless, because they are fully rounded, capable of the thoughts and emotions of human beings in any age.

It is interesting to trace the development of this broadminded, generous-spirited woman. Her life, like Jane Austen's, had three important phases. The first was her childhood and adolescence as Mary Ann Evans. This was followed by the journalistic, social and literary experiences of Marian Evans, and from these the novelist, George Eliot gradually developed.

Mary Ann Evans was born and brought up in Warwickshire. Her father, Robert Evans, an important influence in her life, was for some years a farmer and later a manager on a large local estate. Mary Ann was the youngest of three children and passionately loved her brother Isaac, three years older than herself. They enjoyed a happy home life, though Mary Ann, from an early age, showed a highly sensitive, even passionate temperament. She had sudden moods of ecstatic delight which were swiftly followed by ones of the deepest dejection.

She did not show any special promise of ability at school, indeed she was rather slow, but she enjoyed her schooldays. She went as a boarder to two very different schools, both excellent in their way. At one she was taught the faith of the Anglican Church, with which she was already familiar, and at the other a Nonconformist viewpoint, as well as the usual subjects.

When she was sixteen her mother died. Because her elder sister had recently married and left home, Mary Ann—or Marian, as she preferred to be called—ran the household for her father and brother. This change showed up one of her chief qualities, a firm sense of duty. Nothing was ever too much trouble. But she was very determined to continue her studies. She had a tutor from nearby Coventry for lessons in Italian and German and another for music. She recognised her intellectual powers, wanting to use and extend them further. She read widely and, like the Brontës, constantly. She learnt nine languages using them to read an even wider range of subjects. But there was no one with whom she could exchange ideas. Her life was solitary, and she began to believe that only the serious things of life were important. She suppressed her love of music and literature for a while, deliberately withdrawing into a rigid routine of hard work and religious exercises which brought neither fulfilment nor joy.

Fortunately, after a time, she realised her mistake and gradually came to a greater maturity of thought and judgment. She turned again to literature and music for pleasure and relaxation and by the time she was twenty she had achieved a greater peace of mind. She could now look with greater confidence and interest at her fellow-creatures though, throughout her life, she remained both shy and reserved.

In 1841 Marian and her father moved to Coventry, which was the start of the second important stage in her life. There she found what she had needed, friends with tastes and abilities like her own. In the home of their friend, Charles Bray and his wife, she met many interesting people. With the increasing contact with people her powers of conversation and argument developed and she often lost her shyness when deep in some interesting discussion.

She found the conventional Church beliefs and practices in which she had been brought up insufficient to satisfy her ideas. Gradually, she formed for herself a religion based on moral values coupled with broad sympathies and respect for those who did not share her ideas. She was always humble-minded, aware of her own failings and eager to find the best in others. In later life she wrote : 'We may satirise character and qualities in the abstract without injury to our moral nature, but persons hardly ever. Poor hints and sketches of souls as we are—with some slight vision of the perfect and the true—we had need help each other to gaze at the blessed heavens instead of peering into each other's eyes to find out the motes there.'

Her circle of friends widened and she visited Wales, Scotland, the Lake District and London. For three years her father was ill and when he died in 1849, although she was nearly thirty, she felt completely at a loss. She had always been able to turn to him and although they had had one short quarrel when she had changed her religious views, he was always her firm support. She never lost this need for someone on whom to lean. Although intellectually strong, she was unsure and unhappy if uncertain of affection and understanding. She was herself capable of great love and self-sacrifice and always liked to have some object for her devotion.

Her friends, the Brays, took her with them on a European tour and on their return to England she stayed for eight months at a *pension* in Geneva.

Her interest was stimulated by the people she met there and when she returned to England she began to write critical articles on literary and philosophic subjects, for various quarterly reviews. She also used her command of languages to translate important works by European thinkers.

She moved to London where for some years she was unpaid assistant editor to John Chapman, proprietor and editor of *The Westminster Review*. She was a lodger in his house and devoted herself in her usual single-minded fashion to him and his interests. Proud and happy that he needed her, she refused to see him for what he was—a philanderer exploiting her gifts for his own ends. In the end, his wife and mistress joined forces to get rid of this interloper and Marian Evans went back for a time to Coventry.

Chapman, who had not only enjoyed her obvious devotion but had also depended on her wide knowledge and her practical wisdom, was determined to bring her back to London and *The Westminster*. He somehow pacified the two ladies of his household and easily persuaded Marian to return.

For two years she was busy and happy in the company of the many literary and social celebrities known to Chapman. Charles Dickens and T. H. Huxley were regular visitors, also that famous and rather formidable pair, Harriet Martineau and her brother James, the Unitarian preacher.

Miss Martineau, delicate and deaf, was a clever woman with pronounced opinions, particularly on political and social questions and was much in demand in intellectual circles. She wrote dozens of books and pamphlets on subjects normally managed by men— taxation, the administration of the Poor Law and on political economy in general. She was anti-theological and highly critical of anything she disapproved of. Surprisingly, she was also a writer of stories for children, one of which, *Feats on the Fjord,* is still well known. She was essentially kind, but her rather brusque manner of speaking and sometimes also in her letters could, and did, offend some of her literary friends. Charlotte Brontë, whom she once cruelly accused of being coarse, was very hurt by this. With such a character it is understandable that she approved of much of George Eliot's work when it began to appear later on.

One of the people whom Marian Evans most enjoyed talking to was the philosopher Herbert Spencer. He thought her unequalled among women as a thinker and their friends thought that the friendship would lead to marriage. Spencer, however, had other views. Marriage, he said, was a drudgery, and it would have to be someone of surpassing beauty who could attract him into it.

Fortunately for Marian there was also in their circle a friend of Spencer, George Henry Lewes, a dramatic and literary critic. An excellent journalist, he wrote easily and gracefully on a great variety of topics, and his interest in Charlotte Brontë's work has already been mentioned.

When Marian first met him in 1851 she soon began to realise that he was 'a man of heart and conscience, wearing a mask of flippancy'. She learnt the reason for this later. For two years he had been ill as a result of desertion by his young wife. She had run away with his best friend and literary colleague, Thornton Hunt (son of Leigh Hunt), but throughout his life Lewes supported her, their son and her two children by Hunt.

Lewes was thankful to find in Marian one to whom he could tell his troubles, someone to soothe his racking headaches and his overworked and unhappy self. And Marian at last had found someone who needed all the affection and tenderness that she had to give. Lewes, recognising her great gifts of mind and heart, advised her, as Herbert Spencer had already done, to begin to write novels. His belief and his assurances encouraged her, she had found one on whom she could lean.

Legal marriage for them was out of the question, so, in 1854, they resolutely began a new life together which was to last in perfect harmony until Lewes's death twenty years later. She and Lewes regarded themselves as husband and wife, as indeed they were, except in law. Even her relatives and nearest friends were shocked by this, the one unconventional act of her life. But despite this, Marian felt that she had taken the right step. She was prepared for the censure even of those who might have been expected to understand her reasons.

Out of the happiness and security of that 'marriage of true minds' came the person of 'George Eliot' the novelist. Before moving to the third stage of her life, Marian Evans, who was not indifferent to the good opinion of others, wrote to a friend: 'it is not healthy to dwell on one's feelings and conduct, but only to try and live more faithfully and lovingly every fresh day'. With all her

QUILL PENS AND PETTICOATS

intellectual brilliance Marian Evans remained essentially simple and humble.

After a long visit to Germany they returned to live near London and both worked very hard for the *Westminster Review* and *The Leader,* the first critical weekly magazine, which Lewes had helped to found.

Marian had written several short stories with a clergyman as the central figure. Lewes suggested that they should be offered as a serial to *Blackwood's Magazine.* So they sent the first part to John Blackwood with a letter from Lewes, who wrote on behalf of his 'clerical friend'. Later he had to explain that his friend was not a cleric but a writer about the clergy. He also said that because his friend was very diffident and easily daunted he wished to remain anonymous. Blackwood accepted the serial promptly, paid generously and did everything possible to encourage the over-anxious, timid and still anonymous George Eliot. This pen name had been deliberately chosen as strong-sounding and plain.

In 1858, *Scenes from Clerical Life* was published in book form and in 1859 came *Adam Bede.* They both created a great stir as something new in novels and there was much speculation about the identity of George Eliot. In a charming letter about the unknown author, Charles Dickens wrote : 'I am (I presume) bound to adopt the name that it pleases that excellent writer to assume. I can suggest no better one; but I should have been strongly disposed, if I had been left to my own devices, to address the said writer as a woman. I have observed what seemed to me such womanly touches in those moving fictions (*Scenes from Clerical Life*) that the assurance on the title-page is insufficient to satisfy me even now. If they originated with no woman I believe that no man before had the art of making himself mentally so like a woman since the world began.'

Of course, before long, she had to admit her authorship but she disliked hearing both praise and criticism of her novels. It unfitted her for work, she said. 'The only safe thing for my mind's health is to shut my ears and go on with my work.' That, indeed, was made possible for her by Lewes. He honoured her gifts and always made sure that nothing was allowed to disturb her. How different was her splendid isolation from the snatched opportunities of Jane Austen or Mrs Gaskell.

Adam Bede showed fully her skill as a novelist. She observed people closely but, unlike Mrs Gaskell—and Charlotte Brontë to a lesser degree—she did not reproduce them in her books. She created her characters from her observations and her imagination. In *Adam Bede* she used a tale told by her aunt of a young girl who had been hanged for the murder of her child. The aunt had comforted the young mother before and after her trial as, in the novel, Dinah Morris did for Hetty. George Eliot said, 'Dinah Morris grew out of my recollections of my aunt, but Dinah is not at all like my aunt, who was a very small, black-eyed woman and (as I was told, for I never heard her preach) very vehement in her style of preaching.' This is, of course, very different from the descriptions of Dinah. Similarly, she said, 'Adam (Bede) is not my father any more than Dinah is my aunt. Indeed there is not a single portrait in *Adam Bede*; only the suggestions of experience wrought up into new combinations.'

The main theme of *Adam Bede* is the tragic love story of Hetty Sorrel and Arthur Donnithorne. Their pathetic snatch at happiness in its web of deceit brought misery not only to themselves but to those who loved them like Adam, who said, 'There's a sort of wrong that can never be made up for.' Hetty was transported for life and Arthur spent a lifetime of remorse and repentance for his selfishness, a sad waste of young life and happiness. But it is clearly brought out that the suffering was the inevitable outcome of the sin of self-indulgence and indifference to the feelings of others.

The novel has other, happier characters, the sturdy people of her own Warwickshire villages, who give it a real country atmosphere. Often the author is at her best when portraying these minor characters who are described with the deft touch of affectionate irony so often found in Jane Austen and Mrs Gaskell.

Of these, Mrs Poyser is typical. Here she is in conversation with Squire Donnithorne, who had arrived on horseback at his tenant's farm.

' "Good day, Mrs Poyser," said the old squire, peering at her with his short-sighted eyes—a mode of looking at her which, as Mrs Poyser observed, "allus aggravated her; it was as if you was an insect, and he was going to dab his fingernail on you". However, she said, "Your servant, sir," and curtsied with an air of perfect deference as she advanced towards him. She was not the woman to misbehave towards her betters and fly in the face of the catechism, without severe provocation.

' "Is your husband at home, Mrs Poyser?"

' "Yes, sir; he's only i' the rick-yard. I'll send for him in a minute if you'll please to get down and step in. . . . Hetty, run and tell your uncle to come in," and the old gentleman bowed low in answer to Hetty's curtsy; while Totty, conscious of a pinafore stained with gooseberry jam, stood hiding her face against the clock and peeping round furtively.

' "What a fine old kitchen this is!" said Mr Donnithorne, looking round admiringly. He always spoke in the same deliberate, well-chiselled, polite way, whether his words were sugary or venomous. "And you keep it so exquisitely clean, Mrs Poyser. I like these premises, do you know, beyond any on the estate."

' "Well, sir, since you're fond of 'em, I should be glad if you'd let a bit of repairs be done to 'em, for the boarding's i' that state, as we're like to be eaten up wi' rats and mice; and the cellar, you may stan' up to your knees i' water in't, if you like to go down; but perhaps you'd rather believe my words. Would you please to sit down, sir?"

' "Not yet; I must see your dairy. I have not seen it for years, and I hear on all hands about your fine cheese and butter," said the squire, looking politely unconscious that there could be any question on which he and Mrs Poyser might happen to disagree. "I think I see the door open, there; you must not be surprised if I cast a covetous eye on your cream and butter. I don't expect that Mrs Satchell's cream and butter will bear comparison with yours."

' "I can't say, sir, I'm sure. It's seldom I see other folks's butter, though there's some on it as one's no need to see—the smell's enough. . . ."

'Mr Poyser had just entered in shirt-sleeves and open waistcoat, with a face a shade redder than usual, from the exertion of "pitching". As he stood, red, rotund and radiant, before the small, wiry, cool old gentleman, he looked like a prize apple by the side of a withered crab.'

After *Adam Bede* came *The Mill on the Floss,* also set in the Midland countryside as it was before the Industrial Revolution. It is a story of a brother and sister, Tom and Maggie Tulliver, whose youthful alliance was broken by the circumstances of later life and renewed in their tragic death. In it there is much of Marian Evans' own experience as a child. She, like Maggie, had adored her brother who had gradually grown cold towards her. Maggie had the wild, even violent, affections and aversions that Marian had known as a child. Her craving for love and approval could only have been described by someone who had experienced it.

Remembering her own hopes that more studying would fill the empty places in her heart, she wrote of Maggie: 'she wanted some key that would enable her to understand, and in understanding, endure, the heavy weight that had fallen on her young heart. . . . And so the poor child . . . filling her vacant hours with Latin, geometry and the forms of the syllogism, and feeling a gleam of triumph every now and then that her understanding was quite equal to these peculiarly masculine studies . . . was as lonely in her trouble as if she had been the only girl in the civilised world of that day who had come out of her school life with a soul untrained for inevitable struggles.'

When Maggie fell in love with Stephen Guest, she was deaf to reason and to her usual thought for others. For it was understood that Stephen would one day marry her cousin Lucy, while Maggie knew that Philip Wakem was in love with herself. The position was intolerable. If she married Stephen she would bring unhappiness to both Lucy and Philip, yet by refusing to marry him she could not bring real satisfaction to anyone. Maggie had her creator's sense of duty, she renounced Stephen, but her problem remained and the situation could in no way be righted. Her death may be tragic, but with her passionate nature there could be no future without the love she had, perhaps mistakenly, set aside.

Fortunately, as in *Adam Bede,* the tragic theme is softened by a background of country and domestic life. Among the entertaining minor characters are Maggie's maternal aunts and uncles, the Cleggs, the Deans and the Pullets. Never far away, they are always ready with comments and advice :

'Mr Pullet was a small man with a high nose, small twinkling eyes, and thin lips, in a fresh-looking suit of black and a white cravat, that seemed to have been tied very tight on some higher principle than that of mere personal ease. He bore about the same relation to his tall, good-looking wife, with her balloon sleeves, abundant mantle, and large be-feathered and be-ribboned bonnet, as a small fishing-smack bears to a brig with all its sails set.'

Silas Marner is a gem among novels. It is short, it has a good story, a wide variety of characters and a natural and heart-warming rural setting. It is also freer than the longer novels from the philosophical and moral asides that sometimes slow up development of the story. However, these asides, characteristic of many Victorian novelists were, to George Eliot, an essential part of her writing.

The story is set in Raveloe, a village of peace and plenty. Here in their womanless, comfortless Hall Squire Cass lives with his two sons. One, the spineless Godfrey, is later redeemed by marriage to a charming and sensible wife. But for the other, the odious Dunstan, crime brings swift retribution.

Also in the village is the splendid company that gathers nightly at The Rainbow. Here one evening the slow tide of conversation is suddenly interrupted by the arrival of Silas Marner. This strange, silent man had lived for some years in Raveloe, mixing with none and hoarding the gold pieces he earned by constant work at his hand-loom, on which he made beautiful linen for the richer house-wives of the district. Early in the story he wins sympathy by the tale of his ill-use at the hands of his one-time friends at a chapel in a town far from Raveloe. He had been wrongly accused of stealing the chapel funds and had left the town, bitter and morose, his faith in God and man destroyed, as he thought.

When he burst into The Rainbow with the cry that he had been robbed of his lovingly hoarded gold it was the first step towards renewing the human contact he had almost lost. The story of how the hard gold coins ceased to matter to him when the golden curls of a child found a place in his heart, and his gradual acceptance into the rustic community is told simply and sympathetically.

Like the other novels, it shows that there is no escape from the results of wrong-doing, but it is seasoned with delightful humour. Once they find Marner is not a forbidding alien but a man in need of their help, the villagers are at their amusing and generous best.

This is a happy novel which is as welcome among the more tragic ones as was the sudden delightful smile that could transform the usually severe face of George Eliot. She was easily depressed and always sure that she could never write anything of any value again. Lewes was invariably cheerful and encouraging and once again she would write.

A complete change of scene is found in *Romola,* but the theme, the conflict between self-indulgence and self-sacrifice, is as clearly presented as it is in *Adam Bede. Romola* is set in fifteenth-century Florence in which George Eliot had discovered a particular interest when she and Lewes stayed in the city on their Italian tour. While there they were invited to meet several well-known English people who lived in Florence, including the Brownings. To the great disap-pointment of Mrs Browning who confessed, 'I love her books', they visited little and spent most of their time collecting material for *Romola.* This long and intricate novel is overloaded with historical trappings which make heavy going for the reader.

Felix Holt marked a return to the English domestic novel in which the author is so much at home. Again there is the drama of conflicting standards; and here, too, George Eliot voices the problem of many middle-class Victorian women—the emptiness of their lives. Charlotte Brontë had already spoken through her characters, Shirley and her friend Caroline, of the need for satisfying occupation. And Esther Lyon is angry with Felix Holt when he loftily remarks that women spoil men's lives because life had to be stunted to suit their little needs. She retorts, 'A woman ... is dependent on what happens to her. She must take meaner things because only meaner things are within her reach.' In the same novel an older woman, Mrs Transome, is understandingly described :

'A little daily embroidery had been a constant element in Mrs Transome's life; that soothing occupation of taking stitches to produce what neither she nor anyone else wanted, was then the resource of many a well-born and unhappy woman. . . . It is a fact perhaps kept a little too much in the background that mothers have a self larger than their maternity, and that when their sons have become taller than themselves and are gone from them to college or into the world, there are wide spaces of their time which are not filled with praying for their boys, reading old letters, and envying yet blessing those who are attending to their shirt-buttons.'

George Eliot's health was very frail. Her long toil over *Romola* led her to say that she had begun the book as a young woman and ended it as an old one. She was also anxious about Lewes, who was delicate, but he was always cheerful and lively. When they returned from Italy they lived again in London where they kept very much apart from social life.

They did, however, give Sunday afternoon parties so that people might see and speak with George Eliot. Lewes took all the responsibility of keeping things going—George Eliot found it all very wearing. She sat in state trying to make small talk with the people who were brought one by one to sit beside her for a short time. But in a small company of friends she could relax because the conversation was real. She also loved to be of use to anyone who asked her for advice or help of any kind and she often helped struggling beginners in the arts with money at critical times.

In 1870 she began what is usually considered her finest achievement, *Middlemarch*. This complex canvas paints a Midland town in the mid-nineteenth century. This was a time of great reform : Parliamentary and local government, railway enterprise, medical and hospital improvements, the housing of workers, education, the position of women. All these George Eliot wove into a novel which is alive, not only with social problems but with human love and ambition, human goodness, human sin and folly and its consequences.

At the centre is Dorothea Brooke, the heroine, who embodies most of the virtues and aspirations of the young Marian Evans herself. Dorothea is unresting in her desire to serve others and finds herself hampered time and again even by those who love her. She marries a pompous, elderly clergyman because she is eager to help him in his researches for his great theological work. She even studies Greek for his sake, all to no purpose. She wanted to build decent houses for the workers on her uncle's estate and was ready to pay for their erection, but could do nothing without her uncle's cooperation and goodwill.

Throughout the novel (originally to have been called *Miss Brooke*), she is portrayed with affectionate irony by her creator, who had the sense of humour which Dorothea lacked. Of Dorothea's earnest preparations to fit herself for service to others, she wrote :

'Latin and Greek seemed to her a starting-ground from which all truth could be seen more clearly. . . . Perhaps even Hebrew might be needed—at least the alphabet and a few roots—in order to arrive at the core of things and judge soundly on the social duties of the Christian.'

How well George Eliot had remembered her own eagerness for learning and her later realisation that education alone could not satisfy her needs. Dorothea has that characteristic in common with Maggie Tulliver.

In direct contrast to Dorothea is Rosamond Vincey, completely wrapped up in her own beautiful self, caring only for luxury and admiration. Dr Lydgate, an idealist who is also a skilful and devoted doctor, has the ill-luck to be fascinated by Rosamond's beauty. He marries her and finds out slowly and painfully how cold and greedy she really is.

It is impossible to give a résumé of so broad and deep a novel as *Middlemarch*. There is too much in it. It has deep emotion, profound thought, tolerance, pity and humour. An example of the last is almost topical : here, talking about the proposed laying of railroad tracks, are two countrymen, Solomon Featherstone and Hiram Ford, the waggoner.

Solomon asked Hiram if he 'had seen fellows with staves and instruments spying about; they called themselves railroad people, but there was no telling what they were or what they meant to do. The least they pretended was that they were going to cut Lowick parish into sixes and sevens. "Why, there'll be no stirrin' from one pla-ace to another," said Hiram, thinking of his wagon and horses. "Not a bit," said Mr Solomon. "And cutting up fine land such as this parish! Let 'em go into Tipton, say I. But there's no knowing what there is at the bottom of it. Traffic is what they put for'ard; but it's to do harm to the land and the poor man in the long run."

' "Why, they're Lunnon chaps, I reckon," said Hiram, who had a dim notion of London as a centre of hostility to the country.

' "Ay, to be sure. And in some parts against Brassing, by what I've heard say, the folks fell on 'em when they were spying, and broke their peepholes, as they carry, and drove 'em away, so as they knew better than come again."

' "It war good foon, I'd be bound," said Hiram, whose fun was much restricted by circumstances.

' "Well, I wouldn't meddle with 'em myself," said Sol. "But some say this country's seen its best days, and the sign is as it's being over run with these fellows trampling right and left and wanting to cut it up into railways; and all for the big traffic to swallow up the little, so as there sha'n't be a team left on the land, nor a whip to crack."

' "I'll crack *my* whip about their ear'n, afore they bring it to that, though," said Hiram, while Mr Solomon, shaking his bridle, moved onwards.'

In 1869 one of the visitors at the Lewes' Sunday receptions was John Walter Cross. He was then twenty-nine and George Eliot fifty. He greatly admired her work and became a regular visitor. When, in 1878, George Lewes died it was John Cross who helped the sorrow-stricken woman to continue a life that she now felt was pointless. Cross begged her, as time went on, to marry him. At first she would not listen, but, more than ever, she needed someone to lean on. Finally she consented and they were married immediately.

Eight months later George Eliot was dead. Her last few months of life had been made bearable, even happy, by the devotion of her husband. Shortly after her death he began to write her biography but was so discreet that much of real interest was left out. Other writers have made up for this and further information has given us a greater understanding of this notable woman and her work.

Highly rated in Victorian days, she has not been popular in recent years, probably because of her zeal to edify as well as to entertain her readers. Her insistence on pointing the moral is not much to the taste of modern readers.

However, it seems that there may be a revival of interest in her work, enhanced by the publication, in 1969, of the first major biography of her for some years. As in all things, the pendulum swings both ways.

Note on Sources

JULIAN OF NORWICH

The manuscript of Dame *Julian's Revelations of Divine Love* is available in an edition by Grace Warrack and published by Methuen. Two commentaries are also available, both entitled *Julian of Norwich,* one by Paul Molinari (Longmans), and the other by P. Franklin Chambers (Gollancz).

MARGARET PASTON

The Paston Letters have been edited by John Fenn and re-edited by Mrs Archer-Hind, and published by Dent in Everyman's Library (No. 752). The spelling is modernised. Other editions include *The Paston Letters,* edited with an introduction and notes by M. D. Jones (Cambridge University Press).

DOROTHY OSBORNE

The original manuscripts are in the British Museum, but *The Letters from Dorothy Osborne to Sir William Temple* have been edited by Sir E. A. Parry and published by Dent in the Everyman's Library. Modernised spelling.

CELIA FIENNES

Christopher Morris has edited *The Journeys of Celia Fiennes,* with an introduction (first published by the Cresset Press, 1947).

FANNY BURNEY

An edition of the Diary is available, *The Early Diary of Frances Burney 1768–78,* edited by A. R. Ellis and published by Bell.

JANE AUSTEN

Apart from the novels, which are the best introduction, a number of other useful sources can be consulted : *The Life and Letters of Jane Austen* by William and R. A. Austen-Leigh (John Murray), *The Letters of Jane Austen* collected by Lord Brabourne and first published in 1884 (John Murray), *Jane's Marriage,* which appears in *The Collected Poems of Rudyard Kipling* (Macmillan), and *A Memoir of Jane Austen* by James Edward Austen-Leigh and first published in 1878.

ELIZABETH BARRETT BROWNING

Reference should be made to *Mrs Browning: A Poet's Work and its Setting* by Alethea Hayter (Faber), and to the various editions of her poems. Her letters, owned by the Library of Wellesley College, Massachusetts, have been edited by Betty Miller, *The Letters of Elizabeth Barrett to Miss Mitford* (Murray). Her *Selected Letters* were first published by Smith Elder in 1897, and edited by F. G. Kenyon.

MRS GASKELL

The Gaskell Letters are in the Brotherton Library of the University of Leeds, and others are privately-owned by the Winkworth Family. Use is made of the Gaskell Letters by Elizabeth Haldane in her book *Mrs Gaskell and her Friends.*

CHARLOTTE BRONTE

The first biography was Mrs Gaskell's *Life of Charlotte Brontë,* but more recent books are *The Brontë Story* by Margaret Lane (Heinemann) and *The Brontës Came Here* by Phyllis Whitehead. Certain letters found after Charlotte's death by her father, Rev Patrick Brontë, are quoted by Clement K. Shorter in *Charlotte Brontë and her Circle.*

GEORGE ELIOT

Two important works are *The Life of George Eliot* by John Walter Cross and *George Eliot: Her Life and Books* (Collins).